FINANCIAL
FREEDOM

FINANCIAL FREEDOM

A Step-by-Step Guide

Jack B. Straus, Jr.

Wolgemuth & Hyatt, Publishers, Inc.
Brentwood, Tennessee

Unless otherwise noted, all Scripture quotations are from the New American Standard Bible, © The Lockman Foundation 1960, 1962, 1963, 1968, 1971, 1972, 1973, 1975, 1977, and are used by permission.

Excerpts reprinted by permission from *Prayer* by O. Hallesby, copyright © Augsburg Publishing House.

"The Ad-man's 23" is taken from D. G. Kehl's article "How to Read an Ad: Learning to Read between the Lies," which appeared in the October 1983 issue of *English Journal*, copyright © 1983 by the National Council of Teachers of English. Reprinted by permission of the publisher and the author.

Excerpts from *The Climate of Monastic Prayer* by Thomas Merton, Cistercian Studies Series Number One (Spencer, Mass.-Kalamazoo, Mich.: Cistercian Publications, 1969), used with permission.

Excerpts from *How Should We Then Live?* by Francis A. Schaeffer, copyright © 1976, used by permission of Crossway Books, Westchester, Illinois 60153.

T. Deal and A. Kennedy, *Corporate Cultures*, © 1982, Addison-Wesley Publishing Company, Inc., Reading, Massachusetts. Pgs. 5 and 16 (excerpts). Reprinted with permission.

Wolgemuth & Hyatt, Publishers, Inc.
P.O. Box 1941, Brentwood, Tennessee 37027.

Printed in the United States of America.

Library of Congress Cataloging-in-Publication Data

Straus, Jack B., 1955-
    Financial freedom : a step-by-step guide / Jack B. Straus, Jr. —
    1st ed.
    p.   cm.

ISBN 0-943497-31-0

    1. Finance, Personal   2. Finance, Personal — Religious aspects
    —Christianity.   I. Title.

HG179.S8453   1988   322.024 — dc19   88-27475

CONTENTS

WHEN THE ENDS REFUSE TO MEET

Have you ever thought that making financial ends meet is not really possible? Perhaps it really *can't* be done and we're just kidding ourselves when we think that there is a reasonable chance to be financially secure.

Consider a typical upwardly mobile middle-class American couple — we'll call them George and Martha. George is thirty-eight and Martha is thirty-six. They have one child, George, Jr., who is seven years old. George and Martha have a combined income of about $75,000 a year. They live in an attractive home worth $187,500. They financed $150,000 of that with a thirty-year mortgage at 10.5 percent. Thus, almost 22 percent of their income goes toward the house payments. Let's say it hits 27 percent when we add homeowner's insurance and property taxes.

They save 15 percent to fund a retirement program. Hopefully, they will be able to retire on 80 percent of their pre-retirement expenses.

Junior wants to go to college so they figure that saving about 6 percent of their income would allow him to go to a fairly decent school.

They have a new car that cost $16,000. Financing it over four years at 11 percent will cost them 6.62 percent of their annual income.

A two-week vacation each year will cost them $3,000 — about 4 percent of their income.

They also have life insurance. Through a combination of different products they have been able to get adequate coverage. Their premiums are 2.26 percent of their income each year. Since both George and Martha work, they will pay approximately 7 percent of their income in employment taxes. They might be able to get by with only paying 13 percent of their income in federal taxes. That's a total tax bill of 20 percent. But that may be low if the family lives in a state with its own income tax.

Now suppose Junior wants a full-time playmate. George and Martha agree. Of course, this new baby will also want to go to college. But since they are starting earlier on a savings program, let's say they just need to put away 4 percent a year.

Now, is it realistic for George and Martha to make it with just one car? Add another 6.62 percent, plus 2 percent times two for auto insurance on both cars. Finally, throw in another 4 percent for car repairs and general maintenance around the house.

We now have a total of 97.5 percent of that $75,000 income spoken for. That leaves 2.5 percent ($1,875) for such *nonessentials* as food, gas, clothing, telephone, utilities, and medical expenses! Obviously we have left out the necessaries like furniture, entertainment, dry cleaning, club memberships, baby sitting, videotape rental, frozen yogurt, and a mobile telephone.[1]

So, what's wrong? If we actually sit down and add up the cost of a comfortable lifestyle and worry-free retirement, it doesn't work. We can't do it. What's the solution?

Most of the answers offered today basically give us the same story. If we pull out a few fancy forms, fill them up with some nice but hopeful numbers, follow some "easy to say but hard to do" systematic procedures, and throw in a little discipline and positive thinking, we can attain financial freedom. Success is ours to command. There is only one way to go—up—and God wants all of us on top.

Unfortunately, most of these prosperity-oriented books and seminars have ignored the reality that you and I have to deal with every day. The fact is, in the past decade, the earnings of young men have fallen by almost one-third, seriously hampering their ability to support families above the poverty level. "Average real annual earnings for men age 20-24 fell by nearly 30 percent between 1973 and 1984, from $11,572 to $8,072 in 1984 dollars. In 1973, nearly 60 percent of young men were able to earn enough to lift a family of three out of poverty, but by 1984, only 42 percent were able to do so."[2]

These families are not even the "George and Martha's" of the world making $75,000 a year. They are families that struggle and scratch for a meager living every day and still come up short. They don't make it to the top. Success is always just beyond their grasp.

But in truth, we are these families. For the vast majority of us, trying to make ends meet financially is a day-to-day battle. The positive thinkers and the gurus of motivation sound great, but in the long run most of us still struggle. The money problems are real and persistent. They don't just go away with a wish or a word.

This book is written from personal experience. For the past several years I have been involved in real estate in Dallas. When oil prices collapsed in the mid-eighties, the Texas real estate market began to plummet as well. Losses piled up. Incomes trailed off to nothing. Most developers who weren't forced into bankruptcy still lost virtually everything they had. And I was right in the big middle of it all.

As these events took place I began to think about their meaning and observe some of the consequences. It occurred to me that the prophets of success were wrong. When the market declined, the Christians were affected just as much as the non-Christians. As a matter of fact, in any broad-based financial reversal, there is no discrimination. When the stock market goes down, both the believer and the unbeliever lose. When incomes fall across-the-board, both the believer and the unbeliever are hurt. When bankruptcy petitions fill the courthouse each month, we are just as likely to see one filed by a believer as an unbeliever. *Christianity is not a vaccine against failure.* It rains on the righteous and the unrighteous alike.

In the midst of these crises I saw any number of encouraging signs. A whole host of believers took a personal interest in the financial setbacks of their brothers and sisters. They prayed with them, they comforted them, and they gave sacrificially of their own resources to help others over the difficult periods.

But I also saw some things that were disturbing. I saw that there were many in our midst who confirmed the old saying: "Nobody likes you when you're down." They didn't provide comfort or help. Instead they reacted with mistrust and self-righteousness;

their tendency was to ostracise, not nurture, the hurting individuals. If the situation degenerated into bankruptcy, there were still those who said taking that route was categorically wrong. As one man said, "I felt like we had the plague or AIDS or something. Nobody talked to us after we filed for bankruptcy." Another one remarked, "The hardest thing is going back to church."[3]

That's a sad commentary, isn't it? The church ought to be a place of refuge—somewhere we can go for comfort and acceptance.

I wrote this book with the hope that it will provide a new perspective on how to *truly* attain financial freedom. It's not just for those who are under the stress of financial burdens now. It's also for the rest of the church and those who are called to help when a brother or sister is in need.

The book is divided into two basic parts. The first part contains chapters one through six. It deals with six areas where I believe we are most affected by society when it comes to our financial lives: work, money, debt, lifestyle, economics, and values. The second part covers four areas where God calls us to be witnesses to a changed life: giving, faith, prayer, and contentment.

What we do with each of the issues can have serious consequences, and I sincerely hope you will give them careful thought. Realistic step-by-step solutions and principles are discussed in each chapter. Also, I have tried to stay close to Scripture and examine the issues in light of Biblical guidelines.

This book should be useful to many types of people in many different circumstances. It is for everyone who wonders where the money went when the end of the month comes. It's for those who feel mastered by debt. It's for those who have tried for years to get ahead financially but haven't seen any progress. It's for those who question the value of their work and ask themselves if they should be doing something else. It is for all of us whose sense of spiritual urgency has been obscured by the constant struggle we find in a world of constant financial pressure.

PART ONE

THE LURE OF
THE WORLD

O N E

DISCERN YOUR CALLING
Work

Few things have the potential to both relieve pressure and create pressure as does work—or rather, our concept of work. There will always be a certain amount of stress associated with any job. Yet, there are deeper, underlying pressures that can create fear and put us in a constant state of anxiety.

This type of pressure affects us all, regardless of our job. How does an assembly-line worker feel when he has worked loyally for twenty years and suddenly finds that his company is bankrupt? He's lost his seniority, his pension, his colleagues, everything—and he had absolutely nothing to do with the company's downfall. He gave the best years of his life to the organization. He came to work when he was sore and sick, when his wife was in the hospital, when his kids needed him near, when his parents were dying—he gave his life for his job. Now he has nothing.

And what about the senior executive who helped make his employer into a major force in the marketplace? One day he goes into his office and finds that the company has been bought out—his services aren't needed any longer. He thinks back to the sacrifices he made—being on the road a thousand miles away when his wife was giving birth, working late and missing his kids' soccer games, cancelling a family vacation because the company president needed him. What's left now?

Then there's the engineer who is supposedly being "groomed for department head." For five years he has been diligently developing a new product that, he has been told, will add 10 percent to the company's sales volume and produce big bonuses for him. But at a directors' meeting the decision is made to scrap the whole project and let the staff go. "This particular product just doesn't fit in with our corporate image anymore," he's told. The engineer has given five of the best years of his life to something that his superiors now see as worthless.

These three employees face some tough questions. What have they been doing with their lives for the last five, ten, or twenty years? What did they sacrifice? Why work? Is there a better way?

The same questions should be asked by each of us. The time to consider them is before unemployment is forced upon us — although some of us may not be able to enjoy that luxury. Regardless of when they are asked, it is imperative that we think through the issues surrounding the area where we spend one-half or more of our waking hours — work.

Why Do We Work?

"What advantage does man have in all his work which he does under the sun? A generation goes and a generation comes, but the earth remains forever" (Ecclesiastes 1:3, 4). Solomon saw work as an endless cycle — a treadmill on which we never get ahead. We get up, we go to work, we come home. We get up, we go to work, we come home. Where does it all end? Is it all vanity?

If Solomon was right, then why should any of us even bother? Why work? There are some Scriptural "givens" that help us to answer those questions and why we should work.

Genesis 2:15 shows us one of the most basic of the givens: "Then the Lord God took the man and put him into the garden of Eden to cultivate it and keep it."

From *before* the fall, one of man's primary activities has been to work. The command to work was not changed by the fall of man. Only the effects of work have changed. But the command of God to work is still central to our existence and purpose.

In Exodus 31:2-6, we are shown some specific examples of why certain kinds of people are called to certain kinds of work:

See, I have called by name Bezalel, the son of Uri, the son of Hur, of the tribe of Judah. And I have filled him with the Spirit of God in wisdom, in understanding, in knowledge, and in all kinds of craftsmanship, to make artistic designs for work in gold, in silver, and in bronze, and in the cutting of stones for settings, and in the carving of wood, that he may work in all kinds of craftsmanship. And behold, I Myself have appointed with him Oholiab, the son of Ahisamach, of the tribe of Dan; and in the hearts of all who are skillful I have put skill, that they may make all that I have commanded you.

God gave these people the skills they needed to perform the jobs He wanted them to perform.

In the same way God has given each of us the skills that are necessary for the work He has for us. It is our responsibility to use those skills the way in which He intended. Our work is a calling and is just as important as the call received by Bezalel and Oholiab. Our skills were given to help us in that calling. Our responsibility is to discern the calling and have the discipline to fulfill it.

Paul gives us a very important reason for our work in two different places. First, Acts 20:35:

In everything I showed you that by working hard in this manner you must help the weak and remember the words of the Lord Jesus, that He Himself said, "It is more blessed to give than to receive."

Next, Ephesians 4:28:

Let him who steals steal no longer; but rather let him labor, performing with his own hands what is good, in order that he may have something to share with him who has need.

Both verses contain a very important concept: the shifting of the focus of work from ourselves to others. For too many of us work is nothing more than our way to earn a living or fulfill ourselves. Our conversations about work revolve around its drudgery, what we don't like about our boss, or how unfair our pay scale is. In some cases we don't talk about it at all because it has no relevance to the rest of our lives.

But work must have relevance to our lives as Christians. Paul does not simply mean that we should work to make money to give to the needy. If that were the case, our goal would be to merely

make money, not make "what is good." Work must be relevant to
the Biblical commands to help the weak.

We also work so that we will not be a burden on others. The
well-known verses of 2 Thessalonians 3:8-10 are clear on this point:

> We kept working night and day so that we might not be a burden
> to any of you; . . . For even when we were with you, we used to
> give you this order: if anyone will not work, neither let him eat.

Another view of work held by many today is that we work so
we can get the time and money to play. Through the security
and salary provided by the job, we are enabled to spend our
nonworking hours playing.

Solomon saw the futility in this theory of work:

> And all that my eyes desired I did not refuse them. I did not
> withhold my heart from any pleasure, for my heart was pleased
> because of all my labor and this was my reward for all my
> labor. Thus I considered all my activities which my hands had
> done and the labor which I had exerted, and behold all was
> vanity and striving after wind and there was no profit under the
> sun (Ecclesiastes 2:10, 11).

Working for the sake of those who come after us is another
perspective. But again, Solomon destroys its validity:

> Thus I hated all the fruit of my labor for which I had labored
> under the sun, for I must leave it to the man who will come
> after me. And who knows whether he will be a wise man or a
> fool? Yet he will have control over all the fruit of my labor for
> which I have labored by acting wisely under the sun. This too
> is vanity. Therefore I completely despaired of all the fruit of my
> labor for which I had labored under the sun. When there is a
> man who has labored with wisdom, knowledge and skill, then
> he gives his legacy to one who has not labored with them. This
> too is vanity and a great evil. For what does a man get in all his
> labor and in his striving with which he labors under the sun? Be-
> cause all his days his task is painful and grievous; even at night
> his mind does not rest. This too is vanity (Ecclesiastes 2:18-23).

These passages apply to our heirs and to those who come
after us in our jobs. If you have a lot of customer contact in your

job, think about all the relationships you've built up over the years. What will your successor do with the relationships you've built for your company? All you need to do is consider the relationships you've had with retailers or suppliers. How many were broken when the business was sold or you had to deal with a new person? All the work that was put into your relationship for that company has been destroyed. He who came later was the fool.

Finally, some people work just for the sake of working. Perhaps this is the most futile reason of all. "Then I looked again at vanity under the sun. There was a certain man without a dependent, having neither a son nor a brother, yet there was no end to all his labor. Indeed, his eyes were not satisfied with riches and he never asked, 'And for whom am I laboring and depriving myself of pleasure?' This too is vanity and it is a grievous task" (Ecclesiastes 4:7, 8). Work for work's sake is surely futile.

So, where does all this leave us, or to restate the original question: Why work? George Mueller, the famous German missionary to England and minister to orphans, said it very clearly in 1845. In response to the question: "Why do I carry on this business, or why am I engaged in this trade or profession?" Mueller said that the most typical answer was: "I am engaged in my earthly calling that I may earn the means of obtaining the necessaries of life for myself and family." His response to that answer is the following:

> Here is the chief error from which almost all the rest of the errors which are entertained by children of God, relative to their calling, spring. It is no right and scriptural motive to be engaged in a trade or business or profession merely in order to earn the means for the obtaining of the necessaries of life for ourselves and family, but we should work because it is the Lord's will concerning us. . . . It is quite true that, in general, the Lord provides the necessaries of life by means of our ordinary calling; but that is not THE REASON why we should work. It is plain enough from the consideration that if our possessing the necessaries of life depended upon our ability of working, we could never have freedom from anxiety, for we would always have to say to ourselves, "And what shall I do when I am too old to work, or when by reason of sickness I am unable to earn my bread?" But if, on the other hand, we are engaged in our earthly

calling because it is the will of the Lord concerning us that we should work, and that thus laboring we may provide for our families, and also be able to support the weak, the sick, the aged, and the needy, then we have good and scriptural reason to say to ourselves, "Should it please the Lord to lay me on a bed of sickness, or keep me otherwise by reason of infirmity, or old age, or want of employment, from earning my bread by means of the labor of my hands, or my business, or my profession, he will yet provide for me." Because we who believe are servants of Jesus Christ, who has bought us with his own precious blood, and are not our own, and because this our precious Lord and Master has commanded us to work; therefore we work: and in doing so our Lord will provide for us, but whether in this way or any other way he is sure to provide for us, for we labor in obedience to him; and if even a just earthly master gives wages to his servants, the Lord will surely see to it that we have our wages, if, in obedience to him, we are engaged in our calling, and not for our own sake.[1]

What Have We Gotten Ourselves Into?

Not too long ago the wife of a friend of mine shared a prayer request at a church meeting. Her husband had been out of work for a little over a month and had come up with a way to be self-employed. That particular evening he was traveling, trying to create more business for his new venture. She asked us to pray for him because he "hasn't had a job, a *real* job, since April."

In this simple yet straightforward statement lies the crux of what may very well be the biggest stress inducer in our lives — our concept of work. Many of us are in a salaried position. Rarely have we considered alternatives and rarely have we dwelled on our own unemployment. As long as the paycheck keeps coming every week or every other week we are content. The job's all right and it pays the bills.

But at the thought of layoffs, cutbacks, or terminations something else happens. Our stomach may tighten a bit, we may complain about headaches a little more often, and we start to wonder about other possibilities. If we really lose our job, the wondering turns to panic. We have to find another job before the money runs out. We have to start getting paychecks again. The focus is the job, a job, *any* job.

That focus has been called the "paid employment ethic," and it can best be summarized as follows by author Tony Walter:

> Having a job has ceased to be a means toward an income, creativity, whatever, and has become an end in itself. Alternative ways of getting by, of being creative or reducing loneliness cannot even begin to be considered. Having a paid job becomes a need which cannot be questioned. No amount of counselling that tries to show alternative ways of attaining the ultimate goal will succeed, because as far as the person is concerned the need, a job, *is* the ultimate goal.[2]

When unemployment figures rise, the physical effects of this kind of philosophy are readily apparent all around us. Anxiety, alcoholism, heart disease, suicides, divorce, wife-beating, child abuse—all are influenced by holding to a belief that the job is everything. Internally, we may feel worthless, frustrated, humiliated, useless, embarrassed, and without confidence. Even in advance of a layoff, the anticipation itself creates stress.

> Blood pressure tends to soar. [There is] more hypertension and gastrointestinal upset. This is the anticipatory stage. People waiting for the shoe to drop experience a great deal of stress. Even as the day approaches some workers believe a last-minute reprieve will save them. They become immobilized by this unreasonable belief and their stress.[3]

A study by a special Congressional committee covering a thirty-three-year period revealed that every 1 percent rise in unemployment results in a 4.1 percent increase in suicides, a 3.4 percent increase in admissions to state mental institutions, a 4 percent rise in prison admissions, a 5.7 percent increase in homicides, and a 2 percent increase in the overall death rate.[4] One prominent psychiatrist believes we see those kinds of results because in

> America we have been telling people that their value as a human being lies in their working ability and industriousness, and now we're not giving them jobs. It follows that being out of work can bring about a loss of self-esteem. Employment provides structure, permitting us to plug into socially acceptable

behavior. If an individual is made to feel useless and worthless, he will feel like killing himself, or others. His internal organs will not function properly. He can become a risk to himself and to society.[5]

Actually, we are telling people that their value lies not just in their "working ability and industriousness" but in their ability to hold down paid employment. The job itself has become the "ends." Consider the former $85,000 a year laid-off executive who now spends his time sending out résumés, making phone calls, and arranging interviews. All his time is spent "looking for a job." Then there is the unemployed architect who says that "the worst time is 5 or 6 P.M. That's when you realize you're not coming home from work, that you are home, when you realize you haven't *done anything* all day." Finally, there's the director of a school's job placement center who sees successful men come into his office and break down in tears. "They don't know what they're going to do with their lives," he says.[6]

Corporate Culture

The unemployed person doesn't know what to do because he has always defined his life by his job. And frequently it's more than just, "I'm an accountant" or "I'm a welder." Now we are just as likely to hear, "I'm an accountant with IBM" or "I'm a welder with Ford Motor." The corporation becomes part of the worker's definition. His identity is bound up in both his occupation and his employer.

At every level of society this kind of role definition is encouraged. Within the corporation, cultures have developed to strengthen the bond between employee and company. Terrence Deal and Allan Kennedy explained the concept in their book, *Corporate Cultures*. They reviewed the American history of these cultures by pointing out that

> the early leaders of American business such as Thomas Watson of IBM, Harley Procter of Procter & Gamble, and General Johnson of Johnson & Johnson believed that strong culture brought success. They believed that the lives and productivity of their employees were shaped by where they worked. These builders saw their role as creating an environment — in effect, a

culture—in their companies in which employees could be secure and thereby do the work necessary to make the business a success.[7]

Today, these cultures instill in the employees a way of life:

People at all stages of their careers need to understand culture and how it works because it will likely have a powerful effect on their work lives. People just starting their careers may think a job is just a job. But when they choose a company, they often choose a way of life. The culture shapes their responses in a strong, but subtle way. Culture can make them fast or slow workers, tough or friendly managers, team players or individuals. By the time they've worked for several years, they may be so well conditioned by the culture they may not even recognize it. But when they change jobs, they may be in for a big surprise.[8]

Here is fair warning for all of us—a job *is not* just a job. Don't take a job simply for the sake of having a job. Investigate the culture. Does that culture share your values? Do you want your opinion to be molded by that particular culture? You must not ignore these critical questions. A job may affect you in ways you may not agree with or like.

The Media's Emphasis

The media also encourage the paid employment ethic. Pick up any major metropolitan newspaper and turn to the business section. You will probably find that 90 percent of all articles about corporations are on large ones with employee bases well over a thousand. I tried it once. This was by no means a scientific study but my random selection chose the October 23, 1986 issue of the Dallas Morning News. There were sixteen articles on corporations. They featured LTV, Lone Star Steel, Gulf States Utilities Co., General Motors, Occidental Chemical, Baker International, NL Industries, Zale Corp., Centex, Warner Communications, Continental Airlines, Tandycrafts, Inc., Hyatt Motels Corp., Digital Equipment Corp. and American Airlines. There was one article on a company with less than a thousand employees—Crutcher Resources had about four hundred. However, it was filing for Chapter 11 and used to have thirty-five hundred employees.

The article about LTV was front-page news. The firm had just won a $3.8 billion defense contract that would keep seventeen hundred workers on the job through the next decade. You don't see small companies or self-employed persons getting that kind of top billing. The emphasis in the media is always on the large company with many employees. That continues to encourage the paid employment ethic.

Ironically, that issue of the *News* did have one article on small ventures. But it showed how the government emphasizes large corporations and puts a premium on salaried work. It focused on the new tax reforms.

Governmental Preference

The Tax Reform Act of 1986 removed some substantial investment incentives for start-up companies. Eliminating the capital gains preference is very negative toward young companies. Under the new law, long-term capital gains are taxed at the same rate as ordinary income. Consequently, investors are more likely to invest in older and larger companies where the risk is less and the income return is greater.

Also, as if to say the paid employment ethic is the dominant view of government policy makers, the new law makes noncash compensations appear less attractive. Stock options have been made less appealing. The regular salary is king.

The constant bombardment from our companies, the media, and the government has firmly embedded the paid employment ethic in our minds. We have gone so far in our acceptance of the philosophy that we frequently are unable to see the utter meaninglessness in many of those salaried jobs.

Honesty and Objectivity Required

At this point we need to be honest with ourselves. It's tough to say that for the last ten years I've been doing something totally meaningless. The job has defined me; it has created my identity. But each of us must have the discipline to step back from our jobs and objectively ask: "What's it all for?"

Too often we can never come to grips with that question until it's too late and we're no longer working. We may be like the autoworker who was laid off after two years. At last he admitted that "the monotony and the boredom were getting to me."[9] But while he was working it didn't matter. He was able to rent his own apartment and buy his own motorcycle.

Again, Walter says it well:

> What is remarkable about most employment today is not how boring or alienating it is, but how workers invest intrinsically boring and meaningless work with meaning. Their identity is so bound up with their role as workers that they make sure they convince themselves that their work is worthwhile—if not intrinsically, then for the money, the perks, or the comradeship.[10]

> Unfortunately, most of us never realize how meaningless our work is until it's too late. We're like George, the forty-seven-year-old senior buyer who was hoping for a promotion when his manager asked to see him. Instead, he learned that a cost cutting drive had eliminated his $35,000 a year job. He had been with the company for nineteen years. George said he "felt like he was a [company] person. I prepared myself for promotion, took seminars and courses. In the end," he added bitterly, "it didn't mean a thing."[11]

Janet's dad spent thirty-four years in a steel mill until it was shut down. She's

> bitter because he went to work every day. He didn't even call in sick on Christmas. He gave it all. He sweated for it all, and it wasn't a sacrifice, it was the right thing to do. He deserved more. It wasn't just a job to him, it was everything.[12]

> Her dad related a poignant story about a co-worker that he once found dead at his desk. He helped the guards carry the body out to an ambulance. As he came back into the mill one of the observers stopped him to talk. A loud, long whistle blew as they stood there. It meant: "Give us an ingot now, we're ready to roll it." He responded, "Look at that, Ross, here's this guy dead here, and we ain't even shut the mill down, we're still rolling ingots, nobody even cares that he's dead. They hauled that guy out and they never lost a minute. To them he's nothing."[13]

> It's the stress of meaningless work—the pressure of holding on to a job just because it's a job—the soul-searching agony of redefining yourself because you've lost your job. The job has become part of your way of life; no, even more, it is your life. No

wonder work creates stress. The job itself is too important. You can't afford to lose it and destroy your identity. You can't afford to lose it at all—you need the job.

Some Alternatives

Work is important—Scripture makes that fact inescapable—but the job may or may not be. How do we resolve this conflict? We must do so by developing a view of work that will not create the kind of pressure and stress that so many of us are under today.

A couple of Biblical passages can help us build this view. The first is a rarely practiced, mostly forgotten principle from the Old Testament. It's from Leviticus 25:1-7 and is worth a long, hard look:

> The Lord spoke to Moses at Mount Sinai, saying, "Speak to the sons of Israel, and say to them, 'When you come into the land which I shall give you, then the land shall have a sabbath to the Lord. Six years you shall sow your field, and six years you shall prune your vineyard and gather in its crop, but during the seventh year the land shall have a sabbath rest, a sabbath to the Lord; you shall not sow your field nor prune your vineyard. Your harvest's aftergrowth you shall not reap, and your grapes of untrimmed vines you shall not gather; the land shall have a sabbatical year. And all of you shall have the sabbath products of the land for food; yourself, and your male and female slaves, and your hired man and your foreign resident, those who live as aliens with you. Even your cattle and the animals that are in your land shall have all its crops to eat.'"

This remarkable concept still holds tremendous meaning today. The land itself was to have a Sabbath rest. Every seventh year the people were commanded not to sow or reap. They could live off the previous year's harvest, but in the seventh year there was to be no organized sowing, reaping, farming, pruning, or gathering.

We don't hear much about the sabbatical year or sabbaticals in general anymore, except perhaps from a professor or an artist who is taking time off to write or think or paint. But we should. The sabbath year was as much for the people as for the land. It can be considered to be telling us that we all need to take extended leaves from our work that can refresh us and give us a new vitality and help put our work in perspective. During sabbatical times we can be more objective about our jobs. We can honestly answer questions like: What am I really doing? What does it all mean?

The Sabbath year may also suggest that there may indeed be long periods of time without work that, we could speculate positively, might be used of God. Consider that your unemployment may actually be a forced sabbatical — a way for God to slow you down and encourage you to think about the kind of work you've been doing. Unemployment is not the end of the world. Losing your job does not mean losing your identity. Realizing these things will drastically reduce stress in your life.

Most important, the year of rest gives us, even as it did the Israelites, a better view of work.

> The decisive factor is not daily work in the field or vineyard, but Yahweh the giver of the land. In this way the sabbatical year speaks even more clearly than the weekly Sabbath of the relativity of all work. The goal of all work, its crown, is rest, the Sabbath before the Lord.[14]

Relieving stress will also mean coming to the realization that all of our culture's maxims about hard work may or may not be Scriptural. Solomon saw "that the race is not to the swift, and the battle is not to the warriors, and neither is bread to the wise, nor wealth to the discerning, nor favor to men of ability; for time and chance overtake them all" (Ecclesiastes 9:11).

Time and providence can completely change our position in work. How hard we work may have nothing to do with getting ahead or holding a job. Our lives can just as easily swing from one extreme to the other (Ecclesiastes 3:1-8). And the larger the organization the less control we have, and the more likely our future will be determined by seemingly chance events.

However, by no means is Solomon saying that we shouldn't work hard. In the preceding verse he says, "Whatever your hand finds to do, verily, do with all your might." We must realize that our work is in "the hand of God" (Ecclesiastes 9:1). When we can do that, another major component of work-related stress will be removed. It's not our work or our job that gets us ahead or makes us fall back. In spite of seemingly chance events we are still in God's hands.

One other way in which stress is created is by the constant striving to fulfill our work-related ambitions. We've *got* to have that raise or promotion. We *must* build our company into a major player in the market. A constant driving to reach these kinds of goals can create tremendous pressures — even more so when we fail to reach them.

God has something to say about this too. Unfortunately, it is very difficult for most of us to take. It has been extremely hard for me, but it's extremely important. If we are ever going to succeed at getting rid of work-related pressures, we have to come to grips with it. Paul writes in 1 Thessalonians 4:11,12:

> Make it your ambition to lead a quiet life and attend to your own business and work with your hands, just as we commanded you; so that you may behave properly toward outsiders and not be in any need.

Ambition is a big topic, and it's not my intent to get into it too deeply. But for our purposes let's just say that any ambition beyond what Paul talks about should be turned over to God and committed to Him. If He wants you to get a raise or promotion, you will. If He wants you to build your small consulting firm into one of the giants in the business, you will. There is nothing wrong with any of these things.

However, our hard work should not be work for a promotion or work for a raise or work to build a multinational corporation with power and clout. Our work is for the Lord and to fulfill the calling He gives us (remember Exodus 31:2-6). Our ambition is for Him and His calling.

Step #1 to Financial Freedom

You should not view the loss of paid employment as the end of the world.

Consider taking a sabbatical from your job to focus on your true calling and work.

Discern your calling and your ambitions and strive to keep them in conformity with each other as you seek financial freedom.

TWO

WHOSE IS IT ANYWAY?

Money

In his book *The Penniless Billionaires,* Max Shapiro relates a sad but graphic story about the ephemerality of financial security. It drives home an aspect of money that we should never forget. The setting is the infamous German hyperinflation of the early 1920s.

Lotte Hendlich was a German widow in her fifties. In 1919 she went to Switzerland to visit her relatives for a few weeks. Her expectations were high as she looked forward to a time of relaxation and warm family conversations. Unfortunately, she was about to have the most disastrous experience of her life.

Almost immediately after her arrival, Lotte broke her hip in a fall. During her long period of convalescence she developed a chronic cough. The doctors soon became more concerned about the cough than the hip, and it wasn't long before they realized she was suffering from advanced tuberculosis.

Her illness dragged on and on. The weeks became months and the months became years. In spite of Lotte's despondency surrounding a seemingly interminable illness, Lotte's relatives remained wonderful comforters. They even insisted on defraying all of her expenses, including the doctor's fees.

Finally, in September of 1923, Lotte was "cured," and her doctors said she was well enough to return home. So after a dismal "vacation" in Switzerland she went back to her native Frankfurt.

A four-year absence can make going through the accumulated mail a nightmare. But for Lotte two letters from her bank told a story worse than a nightmare. The first had been written in mid-

1920 by a junior bank officer who had become her friend. He was writing regarding the 600,000 marks in her bank account. That amount was equivalent to about $70,000 at the exchange rate prevailing in 1919. At that time it was large enough to provide her with a comfortable lifestyle for the rest of her days.

The junior officer advised her "to invest most of the funds in your rather substantial bank account. It is my judgment that the purchasing power of the mark will decline, and I suggest you try to guard against this through some suitable investment which we can discuss when you come into the bank."

The next letter was dated several weeks before her return from Switzerland. It said, "Not having heard from you since our last communication, we have closed out your account. Since we no longer have on hand any small-denomination bank notes, we herein enclose a note for one million marks."

Lotte was starting to panic. She nervously turned over the envelope that had held the letter and one million mark note. With a faint gasp of alarm she noticed that the canceled postage stamp affixed to it was for one million marks. Her bank account had been completely consumed by one of the most destructive hyperinflations in history and could no longer pay for an ordinary postage stamp.[1]

Assumptions about Money and Security

No story better illustrates the truth of Proverbs 23:5 than that of the hapless Lotte Hendlich. "When you set your eyes on it, it is gone. For wealth certainly makes itself wings, like an eagle that flies toward the heavens."

In spite of what our society would have us believe about money, there is no security in it. Our attempts to hold onto our money as a means of security are like holding onto ice. The form can't be retained. It will flow through our fingers unless we are quick enough or shrewd enough or wise enough to adapt. Even then there are no guarantees. A great economic upheaval like a hyperinflation or a depression can completely negate all our plans. A minor recession can throw us back ten years. A glut or extensive competition in our sector of the market can destroy us. Our careers and our fortunes can be wiped out at a moment's notice—and we may not be able to do a thing about it. Remember *Black Monday?* On October 19, 1987, the stock market dropped over five hundred points, and thousands of investors all over the country lost everything they had — millions of dollars — all in a blip of a computer screen.

Solomon has a word to those of us who are counting on money.

There is a grievous evil which I have seen under the sun: riches being hoarded by their owner to his hurt. When those riches were lost through a bad investment and he had fathered a son, then there was nothing to support him. As he had come naked from his mother's womb, so will he return as he came. He will take nothing from the fruit of his labor that he can carry in his hand (Ecclesiastes 5:13-15).

Losing money means losing security. But having lots of money can produce the same effect.

Long ago [the rulers of the world] learned that, no matter how much money was in existence, the needs and desires of people would outrun the supply of money. More money would beget more aspirations. They had found that a moderate amount of money created stability but an abundance of money — although it produced a better living standard initially — soon created difficulties as prices rose. The more rapid the pace of newly created money — whether it was barley, stones, dogs' teeth, or gold — the more rapid was the increase in prices. After a while, more and more people could afford less and less. And finally disorder would break out.[2]

Looking at the problem of too much money, Solomon takes a slightly different approach but arrives at a similar conclusion:

When good things increase, those who consume them increase. So what is the advantage to their owners except to look on? (Ecclesiastes 5:11).

In spite of the inability of money to bring security, our society continues to tell us that it does. At every opportunity we are told to invest for our future security, plan wisely for our retirement years by building our assets, and protect the security of our heirs by buying enough life insurance. The government promises to protect our money through federal deposit insurance programs and assures us it is doing its best to eliminate investments that are just pieces of "blue sky" through securities and investor protection laws. Private insurers line up to sell us peace of mind by promoting their products as ways to keep us from liability suits and from the tragedy of losing our worldly goods.

However, all these people, all these companies, and every level of our government make one extremely important assumption. It is so widely accepted that no one questions it. The vast majority in our society consider it a "given" and would be sorely offended if you challenged it. Yet that assumption *is* wrong.

It's best illustrated by a television commercial for a large brokerage company featuring a popular comedian. After touting the virtues of this particular company and telling us how carefully the firm handles money, he concludes: "After all, it's *my* money."

It's God's Money

Here lies the error. It's not *my* money. It's not *your* money. It's not *our* money. It's *God's* money, and until we come to realize that, money will always be an object of stress.

The stress is created by our urgent attempts to hold onto what we believe is our money or to accumulate more money to buy our pleasure and security. It is a constant stress since we are always trying to protect what we have or acquire more.

Most of us who profess Christ ought to realize that the money is not ours. But it seems that the realization never does quite sink in. Banks, financial planners, and even many Christian "financial gurus" put the emphasis on *our* money. So although they may talk about God's ownership of money, it's *only* talk. With such a great amount of time and emphasis placed on budgeting, saving, investing, retirement planning, and estate planning, the idea that it is really God's money gets lost.

Of course the secular media don't help much. Consider some of the recent cover stories from *Money*, a popular and widely circulated magazine on personal finances: "How to Become Financially Independent — Four Ways to Start . . . Right *Now*"; "Your Safest Investments Now"; "20 Winning Strategies for Your Investments"; "No Guts, No Glory! How to Get Rich in Today's America"; "The New Taxes: What You Should Do Now"; "Going For It All — Winning Strategies for Two-Career Couples Today";

"How to Win Big in Real Estate"; "How to Simplify Your Financial Life." I could go on and on with articles from *Forbes, Fortune,
Changing Times, The Wall Street Journal,* and the daily newspaper.
Our society clearly operates under the assumption that "it's my
money." But for Christians that simply won't do. We must challenge the assumption—first in our personal lives, then in our
church, and finally in our society. And to fully understand why
money is not ours, we need to take an honest look at what the
Bible says.

The God of Money

When the people of Israel brought their offerings to the temple, David prayed over the gifts and asked God's blessing. David's
prayer is a wonderful acknowledgement of God's sovereignty
over money and possessions. It's found in 1 Chronicles 29:10-17:

> Blessed art Thou, O Lord God of Israel our father, forever and
> ever. Thine, O Lord, is the greatness and the power and the
> glory and the victory and the majesty, indeed everything that is
> in the heavens and the earth; Thine is the dominion, O Lord,
> and Thou dost exalt Thyself as head over all. Both riches and
> honor come from Thee, and Thou dost rule over all, and in
> Thy hand is power and might; and it lies in Thy hand to make
> great, and to strengthen everyone. Now therefore, our God, we
> thank Thee, and praise Thy glorious name. But who am I and
> who are my people that we should be able to offer as generously
> as this? For all things come from Thee, and from Thy hand we
> have given Thee. For we are sojourners before Thee, and tenants,
> as all our fathers were; our days on the earth are like a shadow,
> and there is no hope. O Lord our God, all this abundance that
> we have provided to build Thee a house for Thy holy name, it
> is from Thy hand, and all is Thine. Since I know, O my God,
> that Thou triest the heart and delightest in uprightness, I, in
> the integrity of my heart, have willingly offered all these things;
> so now with joy I have seen Thy people, who are present here,
> make their offerings willingly to Thee.

David makes it very clear that *everything* comes from God. In
his prayer, David uses two words packed with meaning: "sojourner" and "tenant." The word "sojourner" comes from the Hebrew
root meaning "guest" or "foreigner." "Tenant" literally means a

"temporary visitor." These words convey the meaning that we have no ownership position or no equity in our money or possessions. We are simply being allowed to *use* them for a time. The attitude that money belongs to us is simply wrong.

In case we stop here and agree that it's not our money but assume that our talents and skills have allowed us to accumulate wealth, we are told otherwise in Deuteronomy 8:11-18:

> Beware lest you forget the Lord your God by not keeping His commandments and His ordinances and His statutes which I am commanding you today; lest, when you have eaten and are satisfied, and have built good houses and lived in them, and when your herds and your flocks multiply, and your silver and gold multiply, and all that you have multiplies, then your heart becomes proud, and you forget the Lord your God who brought you out from the land of Egypt, out of the house of slavery. He led you through the great and terrible wilderness, with its fiery serpents and scorpions and thirsty ground where there was no water; He brought water for you out of the rock of flint. In the wilderness He fed you manna which your fathers did not know, that He might humble you and that He might test you, to do good for you in the end. Otherwise, you may say in your heart, "My power and the strength of my hand made me this wealth." But you shall remember the Lord your God, for it is He who is giving you power to make wealth, that He may confirm His covenant which He swore to your fathers, as it is this day.

God has given us "power to make wealth" in the form of skills, talents, and abilities. Such "power" may be intelligence, certain physical attributes, contacts in the community, salesmanship, the ability to organize, or the drive to succeed. But all these are from Him, and we must acknowledge to Him that they are His gifts.

Leave Something Behind

The principle of God's ownership is also illustrated by two interesting concepts from the Old Testament. The first is found in Deuteronomy 24:19-21:

> When you reap your harvest in your field and have forgotten a sheaf in the field, you shall not go back to get it; it shall be for

the alien, for the orphan, and for the widow, in order that the
Lord your God may bless you in all the work of your hands.
When you beat your olive tree, you shall not go over the
boughs again; it shall be for the alien, for the orphan, and for
the widow. When you gather the grapes of your vineyard, you
shall not go over it again; it shall be for the alien, for the orphan, and for the widow.

A provision was to be made for taking care of the poor and
underprivileged people in the community. Sheaves left by mistake were not to be collected, olive trees were not to be beaten
over and over again until there was no fruit left, and grapes that
were missed the first time through were to remain.

This legislation makes sure that resident aliens, orphans, and
widows, though not owning land for themselves, might nevertheless share in the fruit of the land. The manner of their participation in the fruit of the land would be such that they could
maintain their honor and self-respect. They would not have to
beg or seek a 'hand-out'; they would go into the fields and or-
chards after the harvest, and like the farmer, they would work
for their own small harvest, as they searched and gleaned for
the grain and fruit that had been left there.[3]

Contrast this legislation with the practices of modern business. There is no room for letting a product or service "fall
through the cracks." Every piece must be sold for a profit — every
hour must be billed at prevailing rates — every penny must be
earned. The profit margin is slim and nothing can escape. We
are obsessed with extracting every conceivable bit of profit.
There is little room for compassionate thoughts of those struggling
to survive — the stockholders must be satisfied and the bankers
kept at bay.

Even seemingly progressive corporate projects are often
tainted with a bad attitude. Not too long ago a bank in Virginia
opened a child-care center. The CEO did nothing to hide the
bank's reasons for running the center: "There are no altruistic
motivations. We do everything we do with the objective of profit."[4]
He had to justify his actions by deferring to a profit motive.

No wonder we are under stress. Maintaining the attitude
that nothing can be lost creates tremendous pressure. We have

forfeited the freedom available from an attitude of "leaving something behind." If we could somehow recover then I suspect we would feel less pressured. But how can we recover that freedom?

We are no longer an agrarian society, so not all of us can leave grain and grapes behind. Even for farmers this would result in rotting produce. However, some of our businesses do have products or services that can be shared. Food processors can share some of their products, contractors can give labor or materials, publishers can distribute books, power companies can let some energy go without charge, lawyers can defend clients without charge, and doctors can give of their services. The list could go on and on, and it doesn't take a tremendously creative mind to come up with ideas. It just takes a recognition that our skills, products, and services are not ours. We have a responsibility to the needy. Acknowledging that responsibility and acting on it will free us from the tyranny of "profit margin" pressure. Anguishing over every penny is not the way to attain financial freedom.

The Jubilee

The other concept illustrating the principle of God's ownership is probably one of the most radical in Scripture. At least it seems radical for those of us who are committed to a free-market economy. It is the concept of the jubilee and is discussed in Leviticus 25:8-28:

> You are also to count off seven sabbaths of years for yourself, seven times seven years, so that you have the time of the seven sabbaths of years, namely, forty-nine years. You shall then sound a ram's horn abroad on the tenth day of the seventh month; on the day of atonement you shall sound a horn all through your land. You shall thus consecrate the fiftieth year and proclaim a release through the land to all its inhabitants. It shall be a jubilee for you, and each of you shall return to his own property, and each of you shall return to his family. You shall have the fiftieth year as a jubilee; you shall not sow, nor reap its aftergrowth, nor gather in from its untrimmed vines. For it is a jubilee; it shall be holy to you. You shall eat its crops out of the field. On this year of jubilee each of you shall return to his own property. If you make a sale, moreover, to your friend, or buy from your friend's hand, you shall not wrong one

another. Corresponding to the number of years after the jubilee, you shall buy from your friend; he is to sell to you according to the number of years of crops. In proportion to the extent of the years you shall increase its price, and in proportion to the fewness of the years, you shall diminish its price; for it is a number of crops he is selling to you. So you shall not wrong one another, but you shall fear your God; for I am the Lord your God. You shall thus observe My statutes, and keep My judgments, so as to carry them out, that you may live securely on the land. Then the land will yield its produce, so that you can eat your fill and live securely on it. But if you say, "What are we going to eat on the seventh year if we do not sow or gather in our crops?" then I will so order My blessing for you in the sixth year that it will bring forth the crop for three years. When you are sowing the eighth year, you can still eat old things from the crop, eating the old until the ninth year when its crop comes in. The land, moreover, shall not be sold permanently, for the land is Mine; for you are but aliens and sojourners with Me. Thus for every piece of your property, you are to provide for the redemption of the land. If a fellow countryman of yours becomes so poor he has to sell part of his property, then his nearest kinsman is to come and buy back what his relative has sold. Or in case a man has no kinsman, but so recovers his means as to find sufficient for its redemption, then he shall calculate the years since its sale and refund the balance to the man to whom he sold it, and so return to his property. But if he has not found sufficient means to get it back for himself, then what he has sold shall remain in the hands of its purchaser until the year of jubilee; but at the jubilee it shall revert, that he may return to his property.

The reason God gives for the jubilee is "the land is Mine; for you are but aliens and sojourners with Me." The jubilee was to prevent the concentration of wealth — after all, to the Israelites the land was their capital. Wealth was produced through the land.

After careful consideration, it becomes clear that the concept of the jubilee is both anti-mercantilist and anti-Marxist. It opposes mercantilism by decrying the concentration of assets and wealth in a relatively few monopolies. It opposes Marxism by maintaining the concept of private property and the importance of initiative and productivity.

Thus, the purpose of the jubilee was not simply *material* — to redistribute wealth — it was *spiritual* — to show the people that all land and capital was actually God's. It was to prevent the extreme disparity of wealth and poverty so prevalent throughout history. It was to provoke a gracious, generous, and compassionate approach to our possessions.

It was also an incentive to world evangelism: the growing population of Israel was not to remain bottled up on that tiny sliver of land on the eastern edge of the Mediterranean. Instead, as they were displaced from the land by the jubilee, they were to go out to the "uttermost parts of the earth."

Money and Spiritual Growth

Scripture is saturated with admonitions and illustrations demonstrating the effect money has on humanity. Matthew 19:16-24 relates the story of the young man who asked Jesus what he had to do to obtain eternal life. After Jesus quoted the commandments and the young man told of his diligence in keeping them, Jesus said, "If you wish to be complete, go and sell your possessions and give to the poor, and you shall have treasure in heaven; and come, follow Me" (v. 21). But the young man couldn't do it — he owned too much and was unwilling to let it go.

To this young man, money created an impasse in his spiritual life. His attachment to it would keep him forever detached from eternal life. He couldn't acknowledge that his money was really the Lord's.

In Luke 12:16-21 Jesus tells a parable about a rich man who hoarded his crops so that he could take his "ease, eat, drink and be merry for many years." But God's response was, "You fool! This very night your soul is required of you; and now who will own what you have prepared?" (v. 20).

This rich man had not learned that there was no security in the accumulation of assets. It was his money, and he intended to keep it. But little good it did him. "So is the man who lays up treasure for himself, and is not rich toward God" (v. 21).

The parable of the rich man shows us that money has a way of distancing us from God. "Why do we need God if we have money?" Job saw this and remarked that the prosperous say to God: "Depart from us! We do not even desire the knowledge of

Thy ways. Who is the Almighty, that we should serve Him, and what would we gain if we entreat Him?" (Job 21:14, 15).

With exceptional clarity Moses warned the Israelites of the danger of prosperity:

> Then it shall come about when the Lord your God brings you into the land which he swore to your fathers, Abraham, Isaac and Jacob, to give you, great and splendid cities which you did not build, and houses full of all good things which you did not fill, and hewn cisterns which you did not dig, vineyards and olive trees which you did not plant, and you shall eat and be satisfied, then watch yourself, lest you forget the Lord who brought you from the land of Egypt, out of the house of slavery (Deuteronomy 6:10-12).

Moses' warning is timeless. How often we see promising men and women of God suddenly overwhelmed by their comfort and security. The promise of a mature spirituality is lost, and the prospect of significant advancements in the Kingdom of God disappears.

The Deceitfulness of Riches

Those who have never accepted the Gospel are just as likely to be foiled by money as those who have become believers. Consider the parable of the sower. Some seed

> fell among the thorns; and the thorns grew up with it, and choked it out . . . And the one on whom seed was sown among the thorns, this is the man who hears the Word, and the worry of the world, and the deceitfulness of riches choke the Word, and it becomes unfruitful (Luke 8:7, 14).

Riches are deceitful. They tell us they can buy security, happiness, and peace of mind. They tell us we have power and prestige. They tell us to forget about God—who needs Him with all this money? And the most deceitful thing of all is that they never allow us to rest from trying to acquire more money. "He who loves money will not be satisfied with money, nor he who loves abundance with its income. This too is vanity" (Ecclesiastes 5:10).

All these verses about riches almost make us think that it's not worth it to have a lot of money. It would certainly seem that the risk of a nonproductive spiritual life is greater for the wealthy Christian. It also means that if you see a rich man who is godly, he has surely been given an extra measure of God's grace and power. What was impossible with men has become possible with God (Matthew 19:26).

Because of the dangers associated with wealth, we must be extraordinarily cautious. If you have been given riches, be continually on the alert so that their deceitfulness doesn't snare you. Pray that the pressures of wealth will not turn you away from God. The temptation to forget the source of true security will be intense.

If you are not wealthy, carefully consider any aspirations you have in that direction and the motivations behind them. Paul's instructions to Timothy are explicit on this point:

> But those who want to get rich fall into temptation and a snare and many foolish and harmful desires which plunge men into ruin and destruction. For the love of money is a root of all sorts of evil, and some by longing for it have wandered away from the faith, and pierced themselves with many a pang (1 Timothy 6:9-10).

The ambition to acquire wealth can cause an oppressive bondage. Don't let it seduce you. For Christians it usually comes in the form of a desire to be a giver. We say that we want to make a lot of money so that we can give it away. Unfortunately, most of the believers who have that attitude somehow get sidetracked along the way. Their grand gifts never materialize. In spite of their professed reason for getting riches, their desire remains focused on wanting to make a lot of money. The desire should be to give.

The Pressure of Making Ends Meet

It's one thing to suffer from the pressures associated with all the money we need. It's another to have too little. But that's where most of us are. The vast majority of the world's population can only seem to get by — if that. We live from paycheck-to-paycheck or month-to-month or even day-to-day. We never quite have enough money, or we can never quite make ends meet. Naturally, a tremendous amount of pressure is created. How can we afford to get the car repaired? What about new clothes for the kids? Can we pay the electric bill this month? Can we eat next week?

Consider Tom and Sue of Milwaukee. She's twenty-three and he's twenty-five. They have two children — Joshua, who is two-and-one-half years old, and Melissa, who is one-and-one-half. A third child is on the way. Tom is a machinist. He is technically employed full-time, yet has only worked full forty-hour weeks cumulatively about one year out of the last three. Sue stays at home so she can care for the kids. They rent a small duplex for $280 per month (not including utilities), make car payments of about $100 per month, and pay on a small loan taken out to buy their appliances. They have a savings account that might cover one emergency. They hope they'll be able to buy a house in ten years when Sue plans to go back to work. When things get really tight, Sue just breaks down and has a good cry, which she now does fairly often.

Robin is a young social worker who works a second job about ten hours a week as a private counselor just to afford her one-bedroom apartment and her modest standard of living. She is four years out of college with a master's degree and still has three years left on her school loan. She has a thirteen-year-old Volkswagen that's paid for, but repairs cost about $1,000 a year. It's a real strain to get by.

Kevin and Marta have two children. He doesn't have a college degree, but he has extensive training in his field and recently acquired a journeyman's license. They are struggling, paying bills by the "grace of God," and not saving anything. He is in construction and is laid off for months at a time. Health insurance coverage comes and goes, depending on how many hours of work he has clocked. Marta sews the family's clothes. They depend a lot on "luck" and the thoughtfulness of friends.[5]

These stories illustrate what we already know — it's tough to make it today. After tithing (if we do it), giving anywhere from 15 percent to 40 percent to the government (including social security taxes), making our house and car payments, and buying this week's groceries, what's left? Usually not much. The struggle to make ends meet never seems to let up. We never get a break. If only we could experience just *one* week without the pressure of trying to get by. . . . If only. . . .

Salary outlooks don't appear to be getting much better. From 1973 to 1979, 20 percent of new jobs were for workers earning less than $7,000 a year in terms of 1984 buying power. From 1979 through 1984, 60 percent of net new jobs were for those workers. In the 1973 to 1979 period, 64.2 percent of the net new jobs paid between $7,000 and $28,000 (in 1984 dollars). Between 1979 and 1984, 47.5 percent fell in that range. The middle-income worker is getting a smaller share of the new jobs.[6] We are being forced to adjust.

A Periodic Audit

Many financial experts have offered what appears to be excellent advice about how to make ends meet. But somehow the practice doesn't fit with the theory. The most common advice relates to budgeting. Unfortunately, budgets are notoriously hard to stay within. Just when you think you've made it and there are only two days left in the month, an unexpected expense rears its ugly head. At that point you feel like the comedienne who used to say, "It's always something!"

However, I've found one practical suggestion to be very helpful. Instead of budgeting, try a periodic "audit" of your finances. For two months write down everything you spend regardless of the amount. Let nothing escape your watchfulness. Even if you are driving down the road and throw fifty cents into the toll booth, write it down. *Everything* must be recorded.

At the end of this two-month period, categorize your expenditures. Look at them carefully and see where your money went. I think you'll be surprised. This list of expenditures can give you a place to start. Most people who do an audit like this immediately find ways to save money. You may find frivolous spending, things bought on impulse, or purchases that could have waited. Usually some savings will be produced with the audit.

To keep your spending habits under control, let the audit become a regular part of your financial life. Do it once or twice every year.

Consider Your Ways!

Scripture points out another reason why it may be so difficult to make ends meet. Does this strike a responsive chord?

You have sown much, but harvest little; you eat, but there is not enough to be satisfied; you drink, but there is noi enough to become drunk; you put on clothing, but no one is warm enough; and he who earns, earns wages to put into a purse with holes (Haggai 1:6).

There's never quite enough. It almost seems like our wallets have holes in them!

Haggai tells us that there was a specific reason why times were tough. The Lord said, "Is it time for you yourselves to dwell in your paneled houses while this house [of the Lord] lies desolate? . . . Consider your ways! Go up to the mountains, bring wood and rebuild the temple, that I may be pleased with it and be glorified" (Haggai 1:4,7,8). The people were thinking only of themselves and spending money on their own desires. Because of that, God was creating their financial difficulties:

"You look for much, but behold, it comes to little; when you bring it home, I blow it away. Why?" declares the Lord of hosts, "Because of My house which lies desolate, while each of you runs to his own house" (Haggai 1:9).

The financial difficulties and pressure to make ends meet may very well be God's way of telling you, "Consider your ways!"

Not too long ago a former associate of mine came by to see me. We were in the middle of Dallas's real estate depression. Times were hard and most of us who had been in real estate were struggling just to put food on the table next week. He sat down and began to tell me about his new job and how he hoped to be able to pull himself out of the hole within a few years. But right now his salary was barely enough to cover the mortgage and grocery bills. Then he made a statement that I never thought I would hear from him: "I've been looking for things to do and reading a lot of the New Testament." He was serious too. God was able to get through to him in his troubles, whereas He couldn't previously when the money was flowing.

"Consider your ways!" Financial difficulties are so often used by God to get through to us. The pressure brings us to our knees. The stress prompts us to cry out for deliverance. And that deliverance may not come easily. We may be on our knees for

weeks, months, or even years. But God wants us to learn to deal
with the pressure. He wants us to rely on Him for deliverance
and for continued daily provision.

Trust the Lord to Provide

So what comfort do we have under pressure? First, there is
the knowledge that "the Lord makes poor and rich; He brings
low, He also exalts" (1 Samuel 2:7). Since both our wealth and
our poverty are from Him, we know that in wealth He has given
to us and in poverty He will provide. Consider this story from
Matthew 17:24-27:

> And when they had come to Capernaum, those who collected
> the two-drachma tax came to Peter, and said, "Does your
> teacher not pay the two-drachma tax?" He said, "Yes." And
> when he came into the house, Jesus spoke to him first, saying,
> "What do you think, Simon? From whom do the kings of the
> earth collect customs or poll-tax, from their sons or from
> strangers?" And upon his saying, "From strangers," Jesus said
> to him, "Consequently the sons are exempt. But lest we give
> them offense, go to the sea and throw in a hook, and take the
> first fish that comes up; and when you open its mouth, you will
> find a stater. Take that and give it to them for you and Me."

Look at what happened here. After Peter was questioned
about whether or not Jesus paid tax, Jesus told him to go fishing!
Isn't that incredible? Jesus and His disciples needed money for
the most unavoidable obligation of all, and He said to go fishing
and find the money. Jesus' attitude was almost sarcasm bordering
on flippancy. Obviously, Jesus doesn't think that getting money
is too big a deal. And why should it be since it's all His anyway?

Finally, a wonderful story in the Old Testament poignantly
illustrates the sovereignty of God over our needs:

> Then the word of the Lord came to him, saying, "Arise, go to
> Zarephath, which belongs to Sidon, and stay there; behold, I
> have commanded a widow there to provide for you." So he
> arose and went to Zarephath, and when he came to the gate of
> the city, behold, a widow was there gathering sticks; and he
> called to her and said, "Please get me a little water in a jar, that
> I may drink." And as she was going to get it, he called to her

and said, "Please bring me a piece of bread in your hand." But she said, "As the Lord your God lives, I have no bread, only a handful of flour in the bowl and a little oil in the jar; and behold, I am gathering a few sticks that I may go in and prepare for me and my son, that we may eat it and die." Then Elijah said to her, "Do not fear; go, do as you have said, but make me a little bread cake from it first, and bring it out to me, and afterward you may make one for yourself and for your son. For thus says the Lord God of Israel, 'The bowl of flour shall not be exhausted, nor shall the jar of oil be empty, until the day that the Lord sends rain on the face of the earth.'" So she went and did according to the word of Elijah, and she and he and her household ate for many days. The bowl of flour was not exhausted nor did the jar of oil become empty, according to the word of the Lord which He spoke through Elijah (1 Kings 17:8-16).

The provision was the Lord's, and it certainly was a miraculous one. He delivered Elijah, the widow, and her son.

Step #2 to Financial Freedom

If you don't have enough money, remember that it's not your work or effort that feeds you and pays the bills. It's the Lord's provision and grace.

If your money is hindering your spiritual growth, get rid of it — give it to charity, the church, or others in need. After all, it's not yours anyway.

The two parts of this step will speak to different types of people. But all of us should keep the following prayer in mind as we consider our own financial situations:

Give me neither poverty nor riches; feed me with the food that is my portion, lest I be full and deny Thee and say, "Who is the Lord?" Or lest I be in want and steal, and profane the name of my God (Proverbs 30:8,9).

THREE

A HARSH
TASKMASTER
Debt

When we think of debt, it's not hard to picture an ogre caged up somewhere out in the backyard. Periodically we have to feed him (with our interest payments), and for a long time he's not much more than an annoyance. As long as we keep feeding him we're sure he will stay caged. But little by little our ogre starts to grow. It's hard to notice at first, but before long he doesn't have much room left in the cage. We know we have to get a new cage, but we just can't afford it now. Surely his growth will stop.

One day we walk out to feed our ogre and are startled to see an empty cage. The door is ripped off—the ogre couldn't stand to be cramped anymore. Suddenly we are grabbed from behind and thrown into the cage. The ogre hastily repairs the door and slams it shut. We've been imprisoned by our own ogre.

Although this story is the stuff of our nightmares, it happens to thousands of people every day. We are imprisoned by our debt, and even worse, made slaves to it. It's no longer a pet that was there when we needed it, or merely a little annoyance to be fed every month. It is now a burden and humiliation. In many cases, slavery is not too strong a term to use.

Slaves to Debt

The possibility that debt could create slavery has been well known for thousands of years. A vivid example of what could happen appears in Nehemiah 5:1-5. The Jewish people of Nehemiah's day were crying against their fellow Jews. They had mortgaged their fields and their houses to get grain to live. They borrowed money to pay the tax on their fields. Their children were being forced into slavery, and their fields were being taken over by lenders.

The need for food due to the famine was so great that debt seemed to be the only answer. Yet the end result was slavery and loss of ownership. Ultimately, the people lost their land, were forced into slavery, remained deep in debt, and still couldn't feed themselves.

Nehemiah was very angry. He consulted with the rulers and demanded that the people be given back their children and their land.

What was going on? There was a famine, and obviously the people needed to eat. They thought the answer was to borrow. Many of us still believe in the same answer. I've often been told that debt is a necessary evil and we need it to survive. But for some it becomes a way of life.

If debt doesn't lead to slavery, it can easily lead to poverty. From the beginning God emphasized this fact to His people. When the Law was given, the concept of the year of remission became an integral part:

> At the end of every seven years you shall grant a remission of debts. And this is the manner of remission: every creditor shall release what he has loaned to his neighbor; he shall not exact it of his neighbor and his brother, because the Lord's remission has been proclaimed. From a foreigner you may exact it, but your hand shall release whatever of yours is with your brother. However, there shall be no poor among you, since the Lord will surely bless you in the land which the Lord your God is giving you as an inheritance to possess (Deuteronomy 15:1-4).

At the end of every seven years, all the debts of fellow Jews were to be forgiven. When you stop to think about this, it's a remarkable, even radical, concept. To forgive all debt after seven years would change the face of our society and our relationships. It would go a long way toward eliminating poverty, which seems to have been one of the primary reasons for this law. Debt does have a tendency to create and to abet poverty.

What would happen if we had a similar law in force today? In a certain sense we do. Oddly enough, federal bankruptcy law allows a person to file for bankruptcy at the beginning of the seventh year following a prior bankruptcy. Remnants of the year of remission have been passed down to our twentieth-century legal system. The year of remission is still available to those who need it.

Debt and Power

The relationship between debt and power is sometimes obvious and sometimes odd. We've often heard that if you owe the bank $100, the bank owns you, but if you owe the bank $100 million, you own the bank. Recent events in the financial markets have made the latter much less true. However, there is no doubt that lenders are more willing to negotiate work-outs and restructurings with large borrowers. But even then their structurings have generally become opportunities for creditors to impose their values on borrowers. The best example of this is the international debt and the role of the International Monetary Fund (IMF).

The International Monetary Fund is composed of many nations that are required to contribute their monetary quota to the Fund. Loans made to a country in excess of that quota are conditional, and the country must first agree to an IMF-supervised "austerity" program to reorganize its finances. These programs typically include "cuts in government spending, the elimination of price subsidies, a currency devaluation, higher taxes, and higher interest rates."[1] However, eliminating subsidies can actually mean doubling or tripling the price of food for the urban poor. In 1983, there were riots in Brazil and Chile after the IMF-approved austerity measures were implemented.

In 1977, Egypt was given an IMF loan on the condition that subsidies on basic food products like flour, tea, sugar, and oil be lifted. The government complied, and the day after the new policy went into effect, the prices were raised. The subsidies had been a burden on the economy, but there were also many who depended on them. Without subsidies, people couldn't afford the food. So, the day after the prices went up, there were major riots, plundering, breaking into shops, attacking police, overturning cars, and burning houses.[2]

At a 1986 meeting of Latin American debtors, officials discussed the region's massive foreign debt and the parameters of the latest Mexican debt restructuring. A top strategist in Brazil's finance ministry, remarked, "We think this isn't the ideal solution . . . but we have to accept conditions imposed by the international financial markets."[3]

Debt determines the relative position in regard to power of the entities involved. On the international level, we see the relative positions of countries. On the domestic level, it's not uncommon for a bank to dictate internal policy to corporations and other business borrowers, even to the point of forcing out the old management and putting in their own hand-picked successors.

God warned us that this would happen when He tied debt and power together: "You will lend to many nations, but you will not borrow; and you will rule over many nations, but they will not rule over you" (Deuteronomy 15:6).

The next time you feel the urge to borrow, remember that there is a relationship between debt, power, and control. Let that sink in and make it a factor in your decision.

Interest

One of the major reasons why debt is so oppressive is due to the exacting of interest. Interest charges may actually double or triple the cost of the item.

Take, for example, the cost of a home. Assume that you buy a house for $110,000. After making a $10,000 down payment, you find a lender who will give you a thirty-year loan at 11 percent. Your monthly payments of principal and interest will be $952.32. Over the course of your loan you will have paid back $342,836.42, more than three times the actual cost of your home. If your interest rate on a thirty-year mortgage is 15 percent, you will pay back $455,199.85, over four times the home's cost. The interest expense is devastating.

Because of interest, debt has a tendency to multiply in an almost geometric progression. Eventually there comes a point where it's a struggle just to make the interest payments. Finally, the interest payments themselves are beyond reach.

Once again Scripture has a lot to say about interest. We are told not to loan to the poor at interest (Exodus 22:25; Leviticus 25:36) and not to charge interest to our countrymen (Deuteronomy 23:19). God sees how insidious interest is and how it can create an intolerable burden.

We tend to look at these types of verses as instructions to creditors or as "how to lend" verses. But what would happen if we looked at them from another perspective? What do these verses say to the borrower?

They tell the borrower, especially the poor borrower, to be very wary of debt with interest attached. Interest is the killer in debt, and ironically it goes up as the borrower's ability to repay goes down. In banking parlance this is called the "risk premium." As risk increases, so should the return to the bank. Bankers like to raise interest rates when the credit risk is greater. Unfortunately, the risk premium is often self-defeating. Those who can least afford to repay are charged the higher premium. That's one of the paradoxes of debt — he who has is charged less; he who has not is charged more.

Security

An even greater paradox of debt is the concept of security. We've all heard the saying that a bank will only loan you a nickel if you've got a dime. Or, stated another way, "Why do I need to borrow if I've already got the money?"

Actually, there are times when we don't have the money but we have assets that could be converted into money or when we want to purchase another asset but don't have the actual cash. In return for loaning you the money you need, the bank will take a security interest in some asset of yours. If you are borrowing to purchase the asset, the bank will take a security interest in the asset you are buying. If you ever default on your payments, the bank can foreclose and take the asset back. The asset is the bank's security that you will repay the loan.

Security is a part of debt that we usually don't think much about. Most of us understand that we have to give up something in order to have the use of someone else's money. But security is a very important concept to God. Scripture speaks to the type of security that can be taken and the manner in which it can be taken:

> If you ever take your neighbor's cloak as a pledge, you are to return it to him before the sun sets, for that is his only covering; it is his cloak for his body (Exodus 22:26, 27).

> You shall not . . . take a widow's garment in pledge (Deuteronomy 24:17).

The instruction to the creditor is that certain items should never be taken as security and some should be kept only part of the time. These were items that were considered absolutely essential to life. They were to be treated specially.

Another category of assets that required special care included those essential to someone's livelihood. "No one shall take a handmill or an upper millstone in pledge, for he would be taking a life in pledge" (Deuteronomy 24:6).

The small milling machine was an essential part of the Jewish home. Flour was prepared there in order to make the daily bread. Taking the handmill or even the upper millstone, which was a part of the machine, would create a tremendous hardship for the family. It would mean virtually "taking a life in pledge." The sense of those words is "taking in pledge a means of livelihood."[4]

Fortunately, our bankruptcy laws retain special treatment for certain assets. These assets are called exemptions by the law.

Every state, as well as the federal bankruptcy statutes, has its own list of exemptions. The largest is usually the homestead exemption. In Texas, for example, the homestead can be either one or more pieces of real property up to two hundred acres that are not in a city or one or more lots in a city up to one acre, including improvements. Thus, a home is free from creditors, except the mortgagee, in a bankruptcy proceeding.

There are also personal property exemptions. In Texas it can be property with a value up to $30,000 for a family. Some examples of personal property eligible for the exemption include home furnishings, food, tools, equipment, books, clothing, two firearms, and athletic equipment. You can also exempt two forms of travel such as cars, trucks, horses, bicycles, and so on. And for those who have them, these animals can be exempted: "5 cows and their calves; 1 breeding age bull; 20 each of hogs, sheep, and goats; 50 chickens; and 30 each of turkeys, ducks, geese, and guineas."[5]

Although many of the exemptions and their related laws have been abused, the concept is basically a good one and is certainly Biblical in its attempt to protect particular assets from creditors. One of my lawyer friends has gone so far as to say that he believes the bankruptcy laws are the most humane of all laws.

When you consider how far we've come from the days of debtors' prisons, he has a good point.

The way in which security is chosen is also important to God. The procedure set out in Deuteronomy 24:10, 11 has some important implications: "When you make your neighbor a loan of any sort, you shall not enter his house to take his pledge. You shall remain outside, and the man to whom you make the loan shall bring the pledge out to you." This requirement protected the privacy of the borrower's home and left the choice of the collateral up to him. By following this procedure the creditor wasn't free to roam through the house and say, "Why don't I just take this?" The borrower should have the freedom to choose his security. When he doesn't, that's just one more factor creating stress. He may have given up something that he really needs and is living under the constant threat that he could lose it.

Suretyship

Stated simply, you become surety for someone when you personally guarantee that person's debt. It can take many forms but has traditionally implied promising to pay back someone else's loan if he defaults. You can also be surety for corporate debts by personally guaranteeing a loan to a corporation. Owners of small businesses with short track records are often forced to do this by banks.

Another form of surety is "joint and several liability" in a partnership. Typically, when loans are made to partnerships, the lender requires the partners to be jointly and severally liable. Under that scenario, one partner could ultimately be liable for the share of debt of all his other partners. He essentially becomes surety for his partners.

The book of Proverbs has a lot to say about suretyship. Proverbs 6:1-5 makes a vigorous argument against becoming surety:

> My son, if you have become surety for your neighbor, have given a pledge for a stranger, if you have been snared with the words of your mouth, have been caught with the words of your mouth, do this then, my son, and deliver yourself; since you have come into the hand of your neighbor, go, humble yourself, and importune your neighbor, do not give sleep to your eyes, nor

slumber to your eyelids; deliver yourself like a gazelle from the
hunter's hand, and like a bird from the hand of the fowler.

There is a great deal of urgency to these verses, as if being a
surety is a life-and-death matter. And perhaps it is. The problem
with being a surety is that you open yourself up to the risk of
unconditional and potentially unlimited liability. Because you
have no control over the debtor, there is always the chance that
any loss to you could be catastrophic.

A recent experience of mine illustrates this more clearly. I
had been driving a leased car for two years. There was one year
left on the lease, and I thought I would be better off buying a car
at that point. So I ran an ad in the paper looking for someone to
assume the lease payments. It was a good deal for anyone who
needed a car. The payments were low, there was only one year
left on the lease, and at the end of the term the car could be purchased or left at the dealer with no obligation. The only hitch was
that the new lessee had to qualify as a good credit risk by the lessor.

None of the people who wanted the car could qualify because
their credit was just too bad. When they didn't qualify, they asked
me if they could take the car anyway. They assured me that payments would be made on a timely basis. Fortunately, I remem-
bered what Proverbs had to say about suretyship since they were
really asking me to be a surety for their actions regarding the
car. My answer was no.

The potential liability was clear. At a minimum, they could
miss their payments. Next up the ladder was the possibility that
they could run off with the car at the end of the lease. Or they
could have let their insurance expire, and I could be liable for
damage to the car in an accident. But even worse, I could have
had tremendous liability if someone was injured or killed in an
accident that took place after the insurance had expired. And I
would have had no control or voice in the situation.

Proverbs 11:15 warns us about being surety for a stranger. We
must "hate" it. Proverbs 17:18 instructs us not to become surety
for our neighbor. Those who do "lack in sense." Finally, Proverbs
22:26 makes it all-encompassing — don't be a surety for anybody.

These prohibitions against suretyship teach us that lack of
control is not a great way to go into debt. If you can't control

how the debt will be repaid or if its repayment depends on too many variables beyond your control, don't do it. This is especially clear in regard to suretyship since the guarantor has no control over repayment.

If you have already become a surety, Proverbs 6:3 gives some strong advice on getting out. It may not always be possible, but the strength of these words indicates the seriousness you ought to have about desiring deliverance. "Humble yourself" means "stamp or tread yourself," make yourself "small," or "bestir thyself." "Importune your neighbor" means be "boisterous, arrogant, even bully." Do everything you can to get off that debt![6]

Finally, Derek Kidner, in his commentary on Proverbs, has one other important perspective on suretyship: "Even to the recipient, an unconditional pledge may be an unintended disservice by exposing him to temptation and to the subsequent grief of having brought a friend to ruin."[7] There are no winners in suretyship. Avoid it at all costs.

The Lender

Interest, security, suretyship—knowing how each of these factors can affect you is important. But just as important is the lender himself (or itself, as the case may be). In the past, getting and servicing a loan from your friendly neighborhood banker was often a pleasant experience. You knew him and he knew you. Both of you were counting on the relationship as being an integral part of the loan. If you had problems, at least you had a friend who probably lived down the street from you and was supportive in working with you to figure out a way to repay the loan.

Today, in spite of what lenders would like you to believe, there is no such thing as "relationship banking." Many banks have revolving employment doors, and the officer who made you your loan may be on the other side of the country when payment time comes up.

Even more distant are the credit card companies and finance organizations. How can you really know anything about them other than their names and (hopefully) a toll-free phone number? It's hard to check out a lender and know how he will respond when you really need him.

But knowing your lender is just as critical as knowing what kind of security you will put up. Does he have a track record of working with debtors who are having difficulty? Ask around; make a few phone calls. Find out what other borrowers think about your prospective lender. That's one way to reduce the pressure that might arise in the future.

Now — What Do We Do About Debt?

So far we've seen that debt creates slavery, poverty, and oppression. It determines your relative position in regard to power. Interest charges can be devastating to the borrower, and the type of security given up is critical. Suretyship should be avoided at all costs, and you should be careful in picking your lender. But is debt always wrong? Can we make that argument from the Bible? If not, what is a workable principle?

Currently, there are at least three popular theories of debt floating around Christian circles. First, never borrow. Proponents of this theory show us Romans 13:8 and Proverbs 22:7. Paul writes in Romans: "Owe nothing to anyone except to love one another." Proverbs says: "The rich rules over the poor, and the borrower becomes the lender's slave." The second theory says that we should borrow only to purchase appreciating assets. The third theory tells us to borrow only so much as will allow us to maintain our monthly payments at 10 percent (or below) of our monthly income. Corollaries to this theory substitute 15 percent and 20 percent for the 10 percent figure.

The first theory has a lot to say for it, and I must admit that at times I have felt like shouting it from the tallest buildings — buildings that were probably financed 100 percent and subsequently foreclosed on. We've seen a lot of that in Texas. But upon more sober reflection we realize that this theory can't work. If we intend to be literal, we are faced with a line-drawing problem. Do I borrow my neighbor's lawnmower? (By the way, that puts the neighbor in the position of being surety. Think about who could get sued if an accident happened.) Do I borrow my friend's car or clothes for my two-year-old? How about $5 for lunch? $25? $50? $100? Where do we draw the line? None of us really holds that theory literally.

The second theory is an interesting one, although I've never seen a Biblical explanation for it. It was very popular in the inflationary economy of the 1970s. However, its advocates have been quiet in periods of low inflation or deflation. The theory really says to borrow only for big purchases that are necessary (e.g., house, car, etc.). The problem is that cars were never appreciating assets, and lately we've seen houses depreciate in value. This theory just isn't honest.

The third theory also has no Biblical basis. Furthermore, even its proponents are at odds with one another. Is it 10 percent, 15 percent, 25 percent? Just what did he say? Adherents to this theory usually find that it starts at 10 percent and after trying it for a while, begin to like the 25 percent corollary better. In addition, it's a very difficult one to figure out. Really sticking to it would require constant calculations.

Is there any theory that we can feel comfortable with? I think so.

The primary reason for staying out of debt is so that we will not be enslaved. We've seen how God has emphasized this over and over. Scripture shows us how debt leads to powerlessness, poverty, oppression, and ultimately slavery. Like the ogre described at the beginning of this chapter, it can easily become our master.

Paul writes that "all things are lawful for me, but not all things are profitable. All things are lawful for me, but I will not be mastered by anything" (1 Corinthians 6:12). If debt is going to master you, stay away from it. This will have to be an individual decision. Some people will be able to live with more debt than others. Some will simply say: "I will never borrow." Each individual must realize where on the debt scale he is mastered. Each must decide how much power he is willing to give up by going into debt, and each must determine the risk of oppression he is willing to bear.

But none of us should forget the more practical aspects of debt. Interest does increase cost and can be oppressive. What we give up as security is important. Further, credit cards have a tendency to master us subtly. They seem innocuous, but the charges can build up so easily and quickly that we soon become burdened by the payments.

Because of the easy availability of credit cards and other methods of financing, we are tempted to buy things immediately without waiting on God to supply them. We need to be aware of this aspect of credit and how it can master us.

Step #3 to Financial Freedom

Don't borrow without adequate security. That way, if something goes wrong, you can pay off the debt.

Don't let debt master you. Strive to maintain a feeling of freedom with debt and let that determine the extent to which you allow yourself to go into debt.

What Can I Do Now?

These principles and admonitions about debt are good to start living by if you are not already up to your ears in debt. If you are burdened by debt now and feel its mastery, what can you do?

In many cases credit counseling would be helpful. Good counselors can give solid, workable solutions to the problem. But the solutions won't be easy. They will require cutting back expenditures, getting rid of credit cards, and so on. In a sense, these will be your own self-imposed "austerity" measures. Whether you visit a credit counselor or not, you will have to make some hard choices in order to get out of debt.

If you are so overwhelmed by debt that there appears to be no possibility of repayment, you have basically three choices. First, some creditors may be willing to forgive the debt (or part of it) if you confront them with the possibility of expensive bankruptcy procedures. Second, there is bankruptcy itself. Many people will see this as an improper choice and think you are running away from your debts. But if you have prayerfully considered all options and are confident that this is the only way out, you might think of bankruptcy as your own year of remission. It's your turn to start over.

Finally, don't lose sight of the miraculous power of God to deliver individuals from seemingly hopeless situations. Even with debt it has happened before. Reflect on 2 Kings 4:1-7:

> Now a certain woman of the wives of the sons of the prophets cried out to Elisha, "Your servant my husband is dead, and you know that your servant feared the Lord; and the creditor has come to take my two children to be his slaves."

And Elisha said to her, "What shall I do for you? Tell me, what do you have in the house?" And she said, "Your maidservant has nothing in the house except a jar of oil."

Then he said, "Go, borrow vessels at large for yourself from all your neighbors, even empty vessels; do not get a few.

"And you shall go in and shut the door behind you and your sons, and pour out into all these vessels; and you shall set aside what is full."

So she went from him and shut the door behind her and her sons; they were bringing the vessels to her and she poured.

And it came about when the vessels were full, that she said to her son, "Bring me another vessel." And he said to her, "There is not one vessel more." And the oil stopped.

Then she came and told the man of God. And he said, "Go, sell the oil and pay your debt, and you and your sons can live on the rest."

FOUR

POSSESSED BY POSSESSIONS

Lifestyle

A few years ago a wonderfully entertaining and insightful film called *Time Bandits* was released. It opened with a scene in a typical English middle-class living room. Mom and Dad are watching the television and son Kevin is studying behind them.

The program of the hour is a satirical game show appropriately named "Your Money or Your Life." The grand prize that evening was a "wonder-major-all-automatic-convenience-centerette"—a complete kitchen that "gives you all the time in the world to do the things you really want to do." Its infrared freezer-oven complex "can make you a meal from package to plate in fifteen-and-one-half seconds."

Mom isn't impressed. The neighbors have one that can do the same thing in eight seconds. Dad replies that at least "we have a two-speed hedge-cutter." He also has a digital wristwatch that beeps on cue and sends Kevin to bed.

Kevin's sleep is interrupted by a group of midgets who suddenly appear in his room. These midgets have stolen a map of the universe from the Supreme Being. The map shows the locations of holes in the universe. The holes are gateways to any time in history, and one of those holes just happens to be in Kevin's room.

Kevin is forced to join the midgets when they are suddenly pursued by an image of the Supreme Being demanding that the map be returned. Through the course of the movie they visit Napoleon, Robin Hood, Agamemnon, and the *Titanic*—all in an attempt to get "stinking rich."

As their attempts at being international thieves succeed and fail, the Evil One urges them to pursue the "most fabulous object in the world." To do so they must enter the time of legends and find the fortress of ultimate darkness. The Evil One wants the map since it holds the key to his escape from the fortress.

Eventually they reach the fortress, and to Kevin's shock the Evil One has taken on the appearance of the game show host from "Your Money or Your Life." His mom and dad are suitably attired as the helpers. And to cap it off, the Evil One is touting the wonder-major-all-automatic-convenience-centerette as the most fabulous object in the world.

Kevin knows it's a trap, but the midgets are fooled. When they hand the map over to the host to receive their prize, he turns back into the Evil One. Eventually, the Supreme Being rescues them and destroys the Evil One, but he leaves one small piece of evil behind. Kevin is also left behind as the Supreme Being departs with the midgets.

We are then transported back to Kevin's bedroom. His house is on fire and the firemen are breaking into his room. Two firemen rescue him while his parents stand outside debating whether to go back into the house to save the toaster and the blender. A fireman brings out the microwave and says that is where the fire began. There is still a smoking lump of something in the microwave that looks exactly like the piece of evil left behind by the Supreme Being. Kevin frantically screams, "Don't touch it, it's evil!" But his parents pay no attention. They touch it and are destroyed—consumed by evil.

In Pursuit of Possessions

Too many of us in the West are like Kevin's parents. We are enthralled by our possessions and caught up in the pursuit of consumerism. Acquiring the latest gadget, getting the best innovation, and accumulating more and more of the "good things in life" have become daily motivations for living. Products and possessions and the comfortable lifestyle they bring are consuming us. The desire for more is creating financial binds and pressures that could one day destroy us.

Our generation is certainly not the first to put so much emphasis on material things. Francis Schaeffer pointed out that the lack of a "compassionate use of accumulated wealth" was very prevalent in the Industrial Revolution. "This resulted in the growth of the slums in London and other cities and industrial towns, the exploitation of children and women (who suffered especially), and the general discrepancy between the vast wealth of the few and the misery of the many (whose average working day was between twelve and sixteen hours). Seldom did the church, as the church, lift its voice against such 'utilitarianism' (the teaching that utility is the ultimate appeal on all ethical questions)."[1]

Moving further back to the New Testament era, we read the following in James 5:1-5:

> Come now, you rich, weep and howl for your miseries which are coming upon you. Your riches have rotted and your garments have become moth-eaten. Your gold and your silver have rusted; and their rust will be a witness against you and will consume your flesh like fire. It is in the last days that you have stored up your treasure! Behold, the pay of the laborers who mowed your fields and which has been withheld by you, cries out against you; and the outcry of those who did the harvesting has reached the ears of the Lord of Sabaoth. You have lived luxuriously on the earth and led a life of wanton pleasure; you have fattened your hearts in a day of slaughter.

James's language is unusually strong. There are no exceptions or apologies. He implies that it is inevitable for all rich people to have this attitude. Surely he knows that with God "all things are possible" and in at least some, albeit few, cases, there are rich men and women who are given eternal life. But still James rails at the rich. Perhaps he sees something we don't.

It is not a sin to be rich, and most of us would agree that sin presents itself among the rich primarily from the manner in which it is acquired and the way it is used. But let's add one more point. Alec Motyer, in his commentary on James, quotes A. Barnes as saying that sin also exists among the rich when it arises from "the spirit in which it tends to engender in the heart."[2]

Motyer points out that the phrase "you have lived luxuriously" comes from the word "tryphao," which means extravagant comfort stressing the softness of luxury, and "led a life of wanton

pleasure" ("spatalao") suggests the breaking down of divine re-
straints and going beyond pleasure to vice. "Together the words
offer a picture of a life without self-denial, not necessarily cor-
rupt in every way, but certainly offering no resistance to sin
where there is promise of comfort and enjoyment."[3]

The rich of James's day also lived as if their temporal existence were everything. This is the thought behind, "you have fat-
tened your hearts in a day of slaughter." The people were "like so
many unthinking beasts, luxuriating in their rich pasture day
after day, growing fat by the hour and careless of the fact that
each day, each hour, brings the butcher and the abattoir nearer.
Only the thin beast is safe in that day; the well-fed has made itself ready for the knife. In such a way James saw the wealthy,
blind to both heaven and hell, living for the life, forgetting the
day of slaughter."[4]

The spirit engendered in the heart of the rich was seen by
James to dull the sense of spiritual urgency. They saw no need to
contemplate divine judgment, and their affluence brought insensitivity to the needs of others.[5]

Motyer concludes that "the more we surround ourselves with
possessions which only minister to creative comfort, the less we
are likely to cultivate the spiritual trimness of physique which
keeps us fit in the battle for holiness. Furthermore, when we
allow such wealth as we possess to focus attention on ourselves
and our satisfactions, we are ministering to that spirit of pleasure, desire, and wanting for self which is the root of all unholi-
ness and unfaithfulness to God."[6]

The emphasis on a materialistic lifestyle can be traced back
still further. The book of Amos was written around 760 B.C., yet
the first seven verses of the sixth chapter hardly seem out of place
in a modern sermon:

> Woe to those who are at ease in Zion, and to those who feel
> secure in the mountain of Samaria, the distinguished men of
> the foremost of nations, to whom the house of Israel comes. Go
> over to Calneh and look, and go from there to Hamath the
> great, then go down to Gath of the Philistines. Are they better
> than these kingdoms, or is their territory greater than yours?
> Do you put off the day of calamity, and would you bring near
> the seat of violence? Those who recline on beds of ivory and

sprawl on their couches, and eat lambs from the flock and calves from the midst of the stall, who improvise to the sound of the harp, and like David have composed songs for themselves, who drink wine from sacrificial bowls while they anoint themselves with the finest of oils, yet they have not grieved over the ruin of Joseph. Therefore, they will now go into exile at the head of the exiles, and the sprawlers' banqueting will pass away.

It is generally believed that this was written about forty years before Assyria crushed Samaria's northern neighbor Syria. It was a period of peace and security that permitted Jeroboam II to expand. As the expansion progressed, a lucrative trade and powerful merchant class was built up in Samaria. However, the wealth was not evenly distributed. It remained in the hands of a few who spent it on their own lifestyle and neglected the peasant classes.

Amos condemns those who were at ease and felt secure. They were relaxing on their ivory beds and sprawled out on their couches, ignorant of the ruin prevalent in the rest of the country. The fact that they ate lambs and calves showed that they cared nothing for the future. But they would eventually go into exile. Their day of calamity could not be delayed long.

Motyer's interpretation of these verses puts it well. He says they tell us that "the welfare of the fellowship must always take primacy over the pampering of the self. . . . In these verses it is all a matter of looking after the body — bed and food in verse 4, drink and deodorants in verse 6, and most significantly of all, in verse 5, finding non-demanding ways of filling in time with specious reasons offered for doing so. And all the while Joseph is going to wrack and ruin."[7]

In Amos, the main reason for the peoples' behavior is arrogance (v. 8). Wealth has made them proud, and high living has numbed them to the virtue of humility.

Again, it's not just the people of 760 B.C. who fall to pride. All of us are susceptible, and wealth increases our vulnerability. Amos completes for us the thought that Barnes was trying to convey — pride is the spirit that wealth so easily engenders in us.

When humility leaves us, compassion follows. Our uses of wealth become noncompassionate and selfish. We must have that bigger, newer house; we are attracted to the more luxurious car; the most sophisticated stereo system beckons; the latest clothing fashion is a must; and "premium" ice cream is a temptation we just can't resist. We spend and spend and spend—all on ourselves with no thought toward the hungry and homeless. Pride and arrogance have defeated humility and compassion.

Covetousness

It's one thing to have wealth and the pride that can so easily follow, but it's another to not have money and still desire a lifestyle based on material things. This is the pressure of covetousness, and Scripture has a lot to say about that.

The tenth commandment is very clear: "You shall not covet your neighbor's house, you shall not covet your neighbor's wife or his male servant or his female servant or his ox or his donkey or anything that belongs to your neighbor" (Exodus 20:17).

Typically we think of the Ten Commandments as the *big ones*—the most important laws and the easiest to obey. We don't murder, commit adultery, steal, or lie about our neighbors. Our only God is Yahweh, we haven't made any idols, and we don't take His name in vain. We go to church on the Sabbath and honor our parents. But somehow coveting has slipped through the cracks. We usually admit to it on a small scale, but we certainly don't covet enough to worry about it.

I suspect that if we searched our deepest thoughts and feelings, there are some pretty strong desires directed toward things we would like to have. If we are honest, what we perceive as small-scale coveting becomes a little bigger every time we take a look. We may even find ourselves "boasting of our heart's desire" (Psalm 10:3) to our closest Christian friends.

In our culture the boasting that characterized the wicked of David's day is revealed differently. Overt boasting is generally unacceptable in both Christian and non-Christian circles. Our solution is quite simply to talk. We spend an inordinate amount of time talking about our possessions and what we want to buy next. It may not be boasting, but it's close enough to be an annoyance and a clear sign to others of our priorities.

Small-scale coveting leads to talk, and talk to boasting. Boasting eventually leads to insatiable desire. "All things are wearisome; man is not able to tell it. The eye is not satisfied with seeing, nor is the ear filled with hearing" (Ecclesiastes 1:8).

The signs of that desire are all around us. They are most easily seen in attempts to "live up to our income." When we get raises or sudden jumps in our income, the tendency is to spend rather than give or save. Consequently, we can never free ourselves from acquiring things. If the income goes up, we must spend the extra money. The alternative of decreasing our desires is never considered.

This type of lifestyle creates tremendous financial pressures. We tend to reach a plateau and eventually learn to live there. Sure it may be tough to make ends meet for a while, but before too long we are adept at juggling our expenses. At least we can survive, and there's always the prospect of a raise to bring relief.

But the raise doesn't bring relief. The new money exhilarates us and cries out to be spent. We decide that a little celebration won't hurt so we spend. Unfortunately the party doesn't stop, and before long we're back in the hole trying to make ends meet. A few months later the juggling act starts again, and we wait for the next raise to bail us out. That's the kind of pressure created by living up to our income. Ultimately, insatiable desire leads to idolatry. Paul points that out in Colossians 3:5:

> Therefore consider the members of your earthly body as dead to immorality, impurity, passion, evil desire, and greed, which amounts to idolatry.

Violating the tenth commandment has brought us back around to violating the first and second commandments. We have made other gods and idols for ourselves.

Even when we go to the house of the Lord, our minds are somewhere else. The preaching may have a wonderful message, but we don't hear it because we're thinking about work tomorrow or how to close the deal this week. "And they come to you as people come, and sit before you as My people, and hear your words, but they do not do them, for they do the lustful desires expressed by their mouth, and their heart goes after their gain" (Ezekiel 33:31). Our covetous desires have taken control.

Spending Time with Things

Have you ever stopped to consider how much time you spend simply taking care of your possessions? We buy all these wonder-

ful labor-saving devices and live in our houses that are equipped
to serve us, yet for some reason they demand most of our time.
The lawnmower has to be fixed, the dishwasher is out of order,
the garbage disposal needs replacing, the clothes washer is acting up, the faucet is leaking, there is a hole in a screen, the car
has an oil leak, and on and on. All those things demand time.

I'll never forget one of the most frustrating Saturdays I ever
had. One day I got the brilliant notion that I was going to fix the
leaks in both toilets and install new seats on them. It took me the
entire day to replace the insides and seats of both of them! Ad-
mittedly, I don't have great plumbing skills, but between making
three trips to the hardware store for parts and having the difficulty of removing the old parts, I lost eight perfectly good hours.

I'm sure that all of us can testify to the time spent on things.
If it's not repair work, then cleaning and preventative maintenance demand our attention. We wash cars, mow the lawn,
clean the oven, dust the record player, and clean the tape heads.
Granted, many of our devices are great time-savers. But as we
add more and more gadgets to our lives, we can't help spending
time taking care of them.

The danger comes when the time we spend on possessions
precludes our participation in spiritual activities like prayer,
study, worship, and fellowship. The pressure to keep our possessions in order has become too great.

Jesus told a parable about a man who was giving a big dinner. He invited many people, and when the dinner hour came,
he sent his slave to bring them in. But they began to make excuses. One said, "I have bought a piece of land and I need to go
out and look at it; please consider me excused." Another one
said, "I have bought five yoke of oxen, and I am going to try
them out; please consider me excused" (Luke 14:18,19).

What would Jesus say if He heard these excuses: "I've just
bought a new stereo, and I'm going home to try it out"; "I just
picked up my new car so I'm going to drive around for a little
while"? Obviously, they are ridiculous excuses. But we make excuses like these hundreds of times a year and offer them up as
our reasons for not spending enough time in prayer, or not going
to worship, or not giving away a little more this month because
we needed the extra money for some albums.

Too great an emphasis on worldly goods can be dangerous. "Do not love the world, nor the things in the world. If anyone loves the world, the love of the Father is not in him" (1 John 2:15).

Spending that extra money for a slightly better car or a more elegant house or a newer VCR might have been something God really didn't approve of. "But whoever has the world's goods, and beholds his brother in need and closes his heart against him, how does the love of God abide in him?" (1 John 3:17).

The Cult of Consumerism

Covetousness, the noncompassionate use of wealth, and arrogant spending on ourselves are all fueled by what we might call the cult of consumerism. Understanding this concept and knowing how to fight it can eliminate many of the lifestyle pressures we feel.

America is a consumer-oriented society. Our economic growth is primarily created through consumer spending. Consequently, we are bombarded with efforts to get us to part with our money. Spending on material goods is the engine that drives most major corporations, small businesses, and the various governments through tax revenues collected as a result of that spending. In America, the consumer must be king.

We are urged by advertisers to buy their products. We are sold goods that wear out so we can go back for more. We are enticed to spend on new products with marvelous technological innovations. We are told that we *must* have this item because it's the "in" thing. We are prompted, cajoled, pushed, and pulled into ownership of every kind of imaginable human possession. Consumer magazines tell us what to buy and what to avoid. Consumer-oriented government agencies "protect" us. Consumer organizations give us all the facts about products. Consumer television shows make sure we know what everybody is buying this Christmas. Consumer sections of newspapers fill us in on the latest products. We can't seem to escape the consumer society.

How are we pressured by consumerism, and how can we avoid it? The answer lies in how we are affected by advertising, obsolescence, innovation, status, and ownership. An understanding of those areas will give us more insight into beating consumerism and avoiding the mistakes that even Isaiah saw when he said, "Why do you spend money for what is not bread, and your wages for what does not satisfy?" (Isaiah 55:2).

Advertising

Who tells you when you need something? Whenever I speak on lifestyle pressures, I always ask that question and inevitably a large percentage of the audience answers: television or advertisements. Advertising is the prophet of the cult of consumerism. Through the media we are told what to buy.

In *The Lonely Crowd,* sociologist David Riesman writes, "Why, I ask, why isn't it possible that advertising as a whole is a fantastic fraud, presenting an image of America taken seriously by no one, least of all by the advertising men who create it? Just as the mass media persuade people that other people think politics is important, so they persuade people that everyone else cannot wait for his new refrigerator or car or suit of clothes."[8]

Riesman's view of advertising as a fraud is quite cynical. Economist John Kenneth Galbraith is probably more on target with his thought that advertising is an attempt to manipulate people. "Advertising and salesmanship—the management of consumer demand—are vital for planning in the industrial system. At the same time, the wants so created insure the services of the worker. Ideally, his wants are kept slightly in excess of his income. Compelling inducements are then provided for him to go into debt. The pressure of the resulting debt adds to his reliability as a worker."[9]

Galbraith's picture of advertising reminds me of the popular bumper sticker, "I owe, I owe, so off to work I go." Nevertheless, I suspect his description has a high degree of accuracy. The manipulative and managerial tendencies are clearly present. Consider these words of an executive in the advertising industry:

> The reason Coca-Cola advertises is to maintain or increase a level of awareness about itself among people who know full well it exists and what it tastes like, people whom other beverage makers are contacting with similar messages about their products. Simple information about its existence and its popularity— information that triggers residual knowledge in the recipient

about its taste and other characteristics — is legitimate and sufficient. It does what a salesman would do.[10]

Here then is one major aspect of advertising. We hear about
a product and see it so many times that when we want something similar we reach for what we already know about without
even thinking. After all, advertisers don't want us to stop and
think. If we do, we might not buy.

The Smoker's Delight

One of the most successful ad campaigns in history was waged
by cigarette companies to get women to smoke. A brief look at
what happened can help us since we are confronted with new ad
campaigns every day.

In the early 1920s the American Tobacco Co. hired public relations man Edward Bernays. His job was very clear-cut — get
women to smoke. Bernays started by putting pictures of female
smokers in the newspapers. He hired models to light up in fashionable public places, such as the lobby of New York's Waldorf-
Astoria Hotel. He got debutantes to smoke for free by telling
them it was for the liberation of women. He even sent a contin-
gent of debutantes to an Easter Day parade where they called
the cigarettes they smoked while marching "Torches of Freedom."
There were groups of ads designed to capitalize on different
things. One confronted women's fears of being overweight —
"Reach for a Lucky instead of a sweet." Others played on the
liberation theme. One showed a woman and a man smoking together while surfing.

Another group of ads tried to assure people that their fears of
negative outcomes, however reasonable, were false. Some Lucky
Strike ads tried to show how good cigarettes were to the throat.
One pictured a famous actress saying she insured her throat for
$50,000, and to protect it she smoked Lucky cigarettes.

By the 1930s Bernays had made substantial progress, but
there still weren't enough women smoking Luckies. The problem was that women didn't like the green wrapper. So Bernays
used his fashion industry contacts to make green the color of the
year. Lucky Strike underwrote a charity luncheon given by a society matron. The theme was green. Everybody wore green and

all the food dishes were green — even down to the green pistachio mousse dessert. Sales went up.

Sales continued to increase in the 1940s. Women building bomber turrets endorsed smoking because it "calmed their nerves and allowed them to serve better." Actress Rosalind Russell smoked L&M's because they were "what the doctor ordered." Actress Ann Sothern said, "Because my voice is so important I wanted a cigarette that agreed with my throat . . . I choose Camels."[11]

Those endorsements sound humorous today, but a carefully crafted and persistent advertising campaign had increased cigarette sales to women. We have even seen the introduction of cigarettes exclusively for women.

The cigarette example clearly shows the manipulative power of advertising. As the prophet of consumerism it creates pressures within us to buy without thinking. Author Richard Foster describes well what happens:

> The purpose of all this media bombardment is to increase desire. The plan is to change "that's extravagant" into "that would be nice to have," and then into "I really need that" and finally into "I've got to have it!"
>
> We are taken in, duped, brainwashed. But it is done in such subtle ways that we do not realize what has happened. We think we are wise because we can easily see through the childish logic of the commercials. But the ad writer never intended us to believe those silly commercials, only to desire the product they advertise. And sure enough we buy, because the commercials accomplish their goal of influencing our desire.[12]

Be Sales Resistant

The key to dealing with advertising is to build up sales resistance by stopping and thinking. If you allow yourself to take the time to ask and answer the following questions, your sales resistance will be much higher, and you will not easily succumb to advertising's call.

1. Who is speaking in the ad and is the person (or persons) credible?

2. Is what the speaker saying credible?

3. Who is the ad directed toward and why does the advertiser want to attract that audience?

4. What is the purpose of the ad? (Consider both the obvious purpose and what you perceive to be the real purpose.)

5. What is the central idea or focus of the ad?

6. What are the techniques used in the ad and how are they made to influence your decision? (i.e., attention-getting ploys, nonverbal symbols, information provided, rhetoric employed).[13]

One other point should be added. If we take offense at manipulative and slanted ads, as believers we have a responsibility to refrain from using those products in our businesses. We can't expect others to take our opinions about advertising seriously unless we are willing to operate correctly. George Mueller puts it well when he says that we should not "seek to attract the attention of the world by 'boasting advertisements,' such as 'no one manufactures so good an article,' 'no one sells this article so cheap,' 'we sell the best article in the city,' etc. Suppose these statements were quite correct, yet they are unbecoming for a child of God, who has the living God to care for him and to provide for him, and therefore needs not to make use of such boasting, whereby he may seek to insure custom to himself and keep it from others." Mueller reasons that those types of ads are hindrances to believers "because the Lord sees that they are substituted instead of trust in himself."[14]

Finally, I stumbled upon the following piece, which I found both appropriate and entertaining. It's called "The Ad-man's 23rd."

> The Ad-man is my Shepherd,
> I shall ever want.
> He maketh me to walk a mile for a Camel;
> He leadeth me beside Crystal Waters
>   in the High Country of Coors.
> He restoreth my soul with Perrier.
> He guideth me in Marlboro Country
>   for Mammon's sake.
> Yea, though I walk through
>   the Valley of the Jolly Green Giant,

In the shadow of B.O., halitosis,
  indigestion, headache pain,
  and hemorrhoidal tissue,
I will fear no evil,
For I am in Good Hands with Allstate;
Thy Arid, Scope, Tums, Tylenol,
  and Preparation H —
They comfort me.
Stauffers preparest a table before the TV
In the presence of all of my Appetites,
Thou anointest my head with Brylcream;
My Decaffeinated Cup runneth over.
Surely surfeit and security will follow me
All the days of Metropolitan Life,
And I shall dwell in a Continental House
With a mortgage for ever and ever.[15]

Obsolescence and Innovation

Obsolescence tells us that things wear out. Innovation tells us that things are no longer worth being used because something new and better has come along. Both of them fuel consumerism and urge us to keep buying the same products over and over again.

Obsolescence has long been a part of our society. Many believe that planned obsolescence is a part of product development. Manufacturers see that it is designed into the product so that it will wear out. This insures jobs next year as well as continuing profits for the shareholders.

The idea that manufacturers plan obsolescence is extremely difficult to prove. Consequently, we as the general public don't really know for sure whether accusations that obsolescence is built-in are true. Through the years we have heard rumors or read accounts that might lead us to believe planned obsolescence is part of a great conspiracy. However, when all the facts are considered, it's still difficult to reach a conclusion.

Recently, I did run across one interesting story that lends credence to planned obsolescence in the pantyhose industry. It seems that a company has come up with pantyhose guaranteed not to run.

When this company test-marketed the hose in retail stores in New York, the retailers refused to carry the product because that would mean fewer shopping trips for their customers. So the company decided to bypass the retailers and set up its own marketing organization to distribute the hose. The company also claims that there is nothing magical about making hose that don't run. If that's true, why aren't other manufacturers involved?

Well, even so great a consultant as Ann Landers questioned why such hose couldn't be made. She talked to various and sundry people in the hosiery industry and wrote that she "never heard so much double talk" in her life. One reporter concluded that the "hosiery manufacturers aren't about to kill the goose that lays the golden L'Eggs."[16]

In some industries there may indeed be truth to the planned obsolescence theory. However, since some things do wear out, it would be appropriate to add one more point about lifestyle expenditures: watch out for obsolescence.

Watch out for cheapness too. Being frugal with money doesn't mean always buying the cheapest item. I'll never forget the day my law school roommate bought a pair of gym shorts. He went down to the local five-and-dime and came back with a shiny new pair of shorts. Unfortunately, on his first trip around the block they split cleanly up the side. A cheap price *may* also indicate cheap quality. Experience and a careful eye can help you avoid this pitfall.

If obsolescence doesn't cause the product to wear out, innovation makes us think it is obsolete. A new high-resolution television screen comes out and we are told that we will continue to live in the Dark Ages without it. Cars with computer controlled diagnostics are introduced and we are made to feel that we have to rush out and trade in the old one. Blenders with new features, more powerful dishwashers, and better VCRs all compete for our dollars by touting their innovations.

At times innovation cuts the other way, and companies are reluctant to release new products for fear that they will depress established sales. Consider the digital audiotape. This had been developed and proven for a number of years before the general public was made aware of it. Companies were reluctant to market it because the compact disc wasn't firmly established. "The companies are proud of the new development but are afraid of upsetting sales. Some were reluctant to talk about the field at all, fearing that even news of the new products would cause trouble."[17]

Nevertheless, we must be wary of innovation. All too often it is used as a marketing ploy to influence us to throw out the old and bring in the new. Resist that. Carefully think through innovations and whether or not you really need the new product. Perhaps what you already have will do a fine job.

Status

Consumerism preaches status. Christianity demands humility. The two are absolutely opposed to each other on this point. Arrogance versus humbleness. Vice versus virtue. In no other area do we find as great a gulf between the cult of consumerism and the teachings of Jesus. On this issue the pressures put on us by consumerism are intent and unrelenting.

Paul singled out the women of his day to receive some strong words on status: "Likewise, I want women to adorn themselves with proper clothing, modestly and discreetly, not with braided hair and gold or pearls or costly garments; but rather by means of good works, as befits women making a claim to godliness" (1 Timothy 2:9, 10). Paul was issuing a call for modesty and discretion rather than ostentatiousness and extravagance. No more immodest clothing; no more costly garments.

Unfortunately most commentators have focused on the women in the passage rather than the principle involved. Perhaps that's because an emphasis on the principle makes us feel a little more uncomfortable. The principle applies to all believers, not just women.

Thus, the issue for us today is what constitutes ostentatiousness, extravagance, and status-seeking? We must all answer that, and for each of us, the answer will be different. For some, a particular automobile would be extravagant and should be traded in for a car that is less costly or elitist. For others, a simpler wardrobe would be in order. For still others, the house should be sold, and our witness could be to buck the trend to always "move up." Appliances, stereos, jewelry, furniture, china—we must be honest enough with ourselves to question our reasons for owning all these, but we must also be kind. If reasons are found wanting, it's time to let those things go.

If you don't have the finer things in life, don't desire them. Resist the advertisers who prey on human desires for status. No matter how "convincing" they or your friends may sound, "do not be conformed to this world but be transformed by the renewing of your mind, that you may prove what the will of God is, that which is good and acceptable and perfect" (Romans 12:2). Striving for conformity creates great pressure in the Christian life. Be careful that you aren't taken in by those who seek your conformity and appeal to your pride.

There is another related tendency that we most often see during recessionary periods. Incomes are dropping, yet we don't want our status to drop as well. So, we continue to spend in spite of the fact that the money isn't there. The pressure to maintain a certain social level is still present, and by borrowing in order to spend, the financial stress can become overwhelming. The prophet Habakkuk warned of this:

> Behold, as for the proud one, his soul is not right within him; but the righteous will live by his faith . . . Will not all of these take up a taunt-song against him [the haughty man], even mockery and insinuations against him, and say, "Woe to him who increases what is not his — for how long — and makes himself rich with loans?" Will not your creditors rise up suddenly, and those who collect from you awaken? (2:4, 6, 7)

Be sensitive to your financial position. If the money isn't there, don't spend it and don't borrow it. Things *may* get better, but don't bet on the income. Indeed, borrowing to maintain a lifestyle when income won't support it is nothing more than gambling.

There are three other helpful points regarding our battle against consumerism. The first two are part of George Mueller's ten "means whereby the children of God who are engaged in any earthly calling may be able to overcome the difficulties which arise from competition in business, too great a number of persons being occupied in the same calling, stagnation of trade, and the like."[18] Interestingly, these were written in 1844 and are still just as applicable today.

1. "A believer in the Lord Jesus should do nothing in his calling which is purely for the sake of attracting the world; such as, for instance, fitting up his shop or rooms of business in the most costly manner." An expensive setting simply for the

sake of attracting attention is wrong as it causes us to put our trust in those things and not the Lord.

2. One should not "seek the very best, and therefore the most expensive, situations which can be had in a town or city." We shouldn't seek the most obscure or out-of-the-way place either, yet we should not, in today's vernacular, seek the high-rent district. Doing the latter would be "substituting it for dependence upon the living God for customers."[19]

3. Avoid fashions. Fashions appeal to our desire for status. They also promote a form of obsolescence since last year's fashions are out of style and we are told that they should not be worn. Instead, focus on the object's practicality and use-fulness. Avoiding fashions applies to other areas besides clothing. It's often easier to sell a new house if it's today's style rather than one that's ten or twenty years old. The same thing goes for a lot of gadgets on the market. Don't let the manufacturers dupe you into thinking that style and fashion are the primary considerations.

Ownership

Another great teaching of consumerism is ownership. What good does it do the economy to keep our desires in check and refrain from buying more and more things? What good does it do the economy to borrow something from my neighbor since I'll only need to use it once or twice? It doesn't do the economy any good, of course.

On the other hand, Scripture warns against excessive owner-ship. "Woe to those who add house to house and join field to field, until there is no more room, so that you have to live alone in the midst of the land!" (Isaiah 5:8). Isaiah accused the land barons of wanting to own everything in sight until they lived by themselves in their own little world.

Jesus warns us to be on our "guard against every form of greed; for not even when one has an abundance does his life consist of his possessions" (Luke 12:15). Later, in Luke 16:19-31, Jesus illustrates the potential danger in having an abundance of possessions.

He tells a parable about a rich man who "habitually dressed in purple and fine linen, gaily living in splendor every day" (v.19). A poor man named Lazarus came to the rich man and desired just to be fed the crumbs off his table. After a while both died. Lazarus was carried off into heaven; the rich man's lot was in Hades. The rich man saw Lazarus and Abraham and cried out for mercy. Abraham responded, "Child, remember that during your life you received your good things and likewise Lazarus bad things; but now he is being comforted here, and you are in agony" (v. 25).

The point of the parable is not that all the rich go to Hades and all the poor to heaven. That is not always the case. But Jesus wants us to realize that certain choices made on earth are binding in the afterlife. This particular rich man chose worldly riches, pleasure, and luxury as his own good things to be enjoyed on earth. He chose not to accumulate riches for eternity. He wanted it clear that his possessions were his own, and they were to be used on himself in his life of splendor. He never intended them to be used for the welfare of others, especially Lazarus. Thus, he chose earthly ownership, and that was his reward. So too can we expect our rewards to be only earthly ones if we choose temporal ownership and accumulation.

All this brings us to one final act that we can use against consumerism. As much as possible shed the desire for ownership by learning to use things without owning them. There is no need to go right out and buy everything you think you need the instant you need it. You can rent certain items. Or see if you can borrow it from someone else.

This activity will probably be difficult to implement alone. Ideally, a large group of people or perhaps your church itself could agree to a simple, low-key attempt at common ownership as a first step. Certain items could be put into the pool of commonality, and they could be used on a scheduled basis as needed.

Don't forget that this is not without precedent. The early Christians "had all things in common" (Acts 2:44). We might not be ready for their type of community yet, but the principle of shared ownership is still valid for many types of items.

Conclusion

Wealth and possessions tend to engender in us a spirit of pride. Covetousness and desire lead to idolatry. Spending too much time with our possessions precludes time and energy for spiritual activities. The cult of consumerism is a direct challenge to Christianity. Advertising can manipulate us, obsolescence and innovation attempt to create continuing desires, status is used to motivate us, and we are called to ownership for the sake of the economy. All of this leads us to:

Step #4 to Financial Freedom:

Think! Stop and question your motivation and your need before acquiring new possessions.

FIVE

THE GOSPEL OF SELF-INTEREST

Economics

Tulips found their way to Europe from Turkey in the mid-1500s. At the time, their introduction wasn't extraordinary, and there probably wasn't much attention paid to this new flower. Surely no one could imagine that within a hundred years the tulip would be the subject of the first great financial blowout of modern times.

Shortly after their appearance, tulips became a status symbol of the wealthy in Germany and Holland. By 1634 the rage spread to the middle classes. They had to have tulips, and "merchants and shopkeepers, even of moderate means, began to vie with each other in the rarity of these flowers and the preposterous prices they paid for them. A trader at Haarlem was known to pay one-half of his fortune for a single root."[1]

The mania for tulips started to get out of control. The ordinary industry of Holland was neglected. Regular markets for rare tulips were established on the Amsterdam Stock Exchange and in Rotterdam, Haarlem, Leyden, Alkmar, Hoorn, and other major towns. A single bulb might bring as much as 6,000 Dutch florins. In today's money that would be over $22,000 — an astounding price. One person offered twelve acres of prime commercial land for a *Semper Augustus*. Another bought a bulb for a new carriage, two horses, and a complete set of harness.

"Many individuals grew suddenly rich. A golden bait hung temptingly out before the people, and one after the other, they rushed to the tulip-marts, like flies around a honey-pot. Everyone imagined that the passion for tulips would last for ever." It was reported that "nobles, citizens, farmers, mechanics, seamen, footmen, maid-servants, even chimney-sweeps and old clothes women, dabbled in tulips."[2] Many people sold or mortgaged their houses and farms just to purchase the bulbs.

Greed and the dream of instant riches tend to shorten perspective. The strategy of buying for cash and holding for the long term was forgotten. "Rich people no longer bought the flowers to keep them in their gardens but to sell them again at cent per cent profit."[3]

The tulip traders thought prices would rise forever. A futures market for tulips was established. Sellers, for example, would agree to deliver ten bulbs six weeks after signing the contract.

Finally, the structure collapsed. "The more prudent began to see that this folly could not last forever. It was seen that somebody must lose fearfully in the end. As this conviction spread, prices fell and never rose again."[4] The market value of the *Semper Augustus* bulb plunged from 6,000 florins to 500 florins — a 91 percent drop.

> Many who, for a brief season, had emerged from the humbler walks of life, were cast back into their original obscurity. Substantial merchants were reduced almost to beggary, and many a representative of a noble line saw the fortunes of his house ruined beyond redemption.[5]

Booms, Busts, and Vested Interests

Many speculative manias were to follow and continue to this day. The Mississippi madness in France from 1717 to 1720, the South Sea Bubble in England in 1720, the stock market crash of 1929, the oil glut and real estate depression in Texas in the 1980s — all had the same characteristics. Greed and a desire for instant wealth were the common factors and have always proven to be strong motivators. But each mania had a foundation in economics. None of them could have gotten as far as they did without government working closely with the private banking system to inflate the supply of money and credit.

Cheap money stimulates the economy. Investors are seduced by inexpensive credit and throw good money after bad ventures or good ventures at the wrong time. Businesses start projects that can never be paid off. The general public arrives too late to make money but not late enough to be deceived into thinking they too can amass a fortune overnight. But the credit-based boom is illusory. Distorted judgment and huge losses tend to be the only results.

In seventeenth-century Holland banking was a fairly new business. The banks were a private monopoly chartered by Dutch towns. However, bankers had discovered how to expand credit by lending out money that had been deposited with them. Too much lending created inflation. "The prices of the necessaries of life rose again by degrees: houses and lands, horses and carriages, and luxuries of every sort, rose in value with them."[6] Then came the crash.

The power of economic events to influence our behavior is easily seen in these kinds of manias. But economic theories and practices are just as prevalent in our daily lives. They influence us in subtle ways at virtually every transaction. John Maynard Keynes, one of this century's most influential economists, said that

> the ideas of economists and political philosophers, both when they are right and when they are wrong, are more powerful than is commonly understood. Indeed, the world is ruled by little else. Practical men, who believe themselves to be quite exempt from any intellectual influences, are usually the slaves of some defunct economist. Madmen in authority, who hear voices in the air, are distilling their frenzy from some academic scribbler of a few years back. I am sure that the power of vested interests is vastly exaggerated compared with the gradual encroachment of ideas.[7]

We Christians tend to ignore a discipline such as economics. We rarely give a second thought to the fact that our daily actions might be influenced by theories and thoughts of non-Christian thinkers and their financial systems. Francis Schaeffer was astute enough to recognize that the world's philosophers and their musings can profoundly influence the ordinary believer. To come to grips with why we behave certain ways in regard to money, we must recognize that economists have a similar influence, and we, in turn, are affected by the economic systems we live under.

Our own particular American style of capitalism affects us more than we think. The market drives us to do certain things and act in certain ways, and most of the time we never question our motives. We simply accept the common way of acting in our society and proceed full steam ahead.

In order to understand how we act, it's helpful to first look at another system. It's usually easier to focus on someone else's faults before we turn to our own. This will help us know what to look for when we analyze the American economic way.

Communism

Like Keynes, Karl Marx understood the power of economics to shape a society:

> In every historical epoch, the prevailing mode of economic production and exchange, and the social organization necessarily following from it, form the basis upon which is built up, and from which alone can be explained, the political and intellectual history of that epoch.[8]

Thus, communist party leaders have always sought to shape their society around their view of economics. Whether the man on a Moscow street likes it or not, most of his financial decisions are a product of theories penned 150 years ago.

A central communistic tenet is the abolition of private property and consequent centralization of all instruments of production in the hands of the state.[9] From this basic concept stem a number of different methods to get property to the state and keep it there. Marx started with the following, some of which I have abbreviated or summarized:

1. Application of all rents of land to public purposes.

2. A heavy progressive or gradual income tax.

3. Abolition of all rights of inheritance.

4. Confiscation of the property of all emigrants and rebels.

5. Centralization of credit in the hands of the state, by means of a national bank with state capital and an exclusive monopoly.

6. Centralization of communication and transportation in the hands of the state.

7. Extension of factories owned by the state and cultivation of the soil in accordance with a common plan.

8. Equal liability of all to labor.

9. Gradual abolition of the distinction between town and country by distributing the population.

10. Free education for all children in public schools.[10]

The theory and practice of communism tend to establish the relative value of things through the amount of labor required to produce them. Labor is the key ingredient. As such, work is viewed as being extremely important. It is "the means by which the masses gain collective pride and power."[11]

The emphasis is on "collective." The worker doesn't work for himself. He works for the state, and his behavior is oriented around that fact. Leonid Brezhnev, former General Secretary of the communist party, put it this way: "Under the conditions of socialism, Soviet man has developed what is truly a valuable quality: a sense of being the master of his country who clearly sees the connection between his work and the cause of the whole nation and who always remembers and thinks of common interests."[12]

Obviously, much of the talk about the Soviet worker's concern for the state is rhetoric. We've all read about the extent of the black market in the U.S.S.R. and the difficulty involved in motivating workers to produce their quotas. Yet the communist system does focus on labor for the state. Greater production must further the interests of the state. Technological advancement must contribute to the state.

Those are the fundamentals. From them follows the diversity of what is known as "national communism," the variation of communism from country to country based on national needs and cultural tradition. This is especially evident in some of the African communist movements. They add the concept of African autonomy. The influences of various colonial experiences have taught the Africans that the "crucial issue is not whether the means of production are owned publicly or privately but that they be controlled by Africans who are free of colonial and neocolonial attitudes."[13]

The Eurocommunists are also adjusting the teachings of Marxism-Leninism. They are demanding that each party be free to apply those teachings according to national needs and circumstances.

In the 1960s Cuba tried to create a new economic man motivated purely by moral incentives. The country was not successful, so to induce rural workers to stay on the farm the leaders offered material incentives such as more abundant food than exists in Havana. Other workers received different incentives. These included tickets to the Tropicana nightclub, a week-long vacation at Varadero Beach, a top spot on the waiting list for a new apartment, and various electrical appliances.[14]

All this is not meant to be a discourse on the effects of communism. It's just to show that it can be fairly easy to stand on the outside of an economic system and see how it affects the men who must live under that system. Now we should heed the words of Jesus in Luke 6:41:

> And why do you look at the speck that is in your brother's eye,
> but do not notice the log that is in your own eye?

Communism has many faults that seem clear to us. They are more than just a speck in an eye. But our own brand of capitalism has faults too. Sometimes it's easy to let our national pride and cultural blinders keep us from seeing those. However, if we are to truly understand many of the financial pressures we face, we must take an honest look at our economy and how it influences our decisions.

Capitalism in America

First, we must admit that even as African communists aren't pure communists, American capitalists aren't pure capitalists. We live in a system of mixed capitalism. Pure capitalism says that capital is the principal producer of wealth in an advanced industrial economy. But in our society, human labor is also a producer of wealth. Thus the division into a mixed economy. The stock and commodity traders who are seeking to produce wealth through movement of capital are the purest capitalists. Those without capital who must rely on their labor to gain wealth are at the opposite extreme.

At the governmental level pure capitalism began to decline with the advent of the Great Depression and the prominence of the economic theory espoused by John Maynard Keynes. A little background might be helpful to show how one economic theory can change the course of our government and our relationship to it.

Prior to the Great Depression, it was believed that the capitalist system found its equilibrium at full employment. Idle men were considered unnatural. The Depression destroyed that idea. The capitalist economy could just as well find equilibrium at serious unemployment — 25 percent or greater at the time.

It was then believed that the underemployment was caused by businesses and individuals saving more than was currently profitable for businesses to invest. What was saved must ultimately be spent or there would be a shortage of purchasing power. In the short term, savings were always invested. If there was a surplus of savings, interest rates would fall, insuring the use of the money.

Keynes showed that economic slumps reduced both investment and savings. Thus, employment remained low. Keynes proposed that the government should borrow and invest. If the government borrowed and invested enough, savings would be offset by investment at a higher level of output. Employment would then go up. Here began the idea of government spending to create jobs and the movement away from capitalism.

Since that time we have come a long way. Government expenditures have skyrocketed. Whether right or wrong more people depend on the government for their financial security than ever. It has become their security blanket.

In 1977 I had the opportunity to work for a congressman on Capitol Hill. One of my duties was to review pending legislation, analyze it from all sides, present supporting data for each position, and finally give my recommendation. One day the congressman was in a rush to get to the floor to vote on a relatively minor bill. Since the vote was approaching we discussed the bill in the elevator. My conclusion was that a "no" vote was in order. My reason — it's just one more step down the road to socialism. As I said that he turned around and looked me right in the eye. I don't remember the subject of the bill, but I'll never forget his response to my reasoning: "Jack, we're already there."

Whether we realize it, like it, or even care about it, economic theories have changed our lives. It is essential that we understand them and their influence which will in turn give us greater discipline in our personal financial lives and create a greater awareness of how changes in economic policies can ultimately affect us.

Capitalism and Work

In 1776 Adam Smith published what would eventually become the cornerstone of capitalist economic thought titled "An Inquiry into the Nature and Causes of the Wealth of Nations." His analysis of where wealth comes from continues as virtual undisputed dogma in our system today. Smith said that "the wealth of a nation results from the diligent pursuit by each of its citizens of his own interests — when he reaps the resulting reward or suffers any resulting penalties. In serving his own interests, the individual serves the public interests." John Galbraith accurately summed up our commitment to this idea when he noted that "self-interest and freedom of enterprise were a secular faith in the Old World. In the New World they emerged as religion."[15]

This theory has unquestionably had tremendous success in creating wealth. By pursuing our own self-interest, we Americans have produced the richest economy in the history of this planet. More people than at any other point in history have been able to live under extraordinarily prosperous conditions. We speak of the German and Japanese miracles after World War II. We point to the colonial empires built by England and Spain. We marvel at the wonders produced by ancient Rome and Greece. Yet no country or empire can boast of the astounding economic advancements achieved by the United States of America.

The System in Operation

With that in mind, it is not my intent to pass judgment on the economic system we live under. Systems themselves are amoral and I am convinced that most any system can supply the needs of its people in a humane way if the right leadership is in power. The key is not the system but the leadership. Nevertheless, every system lends itself to certain abuses that result in ungodly practices. When we are operating within a system, it becomes difficult to honestly evaluate the abuses.

As Christians we must periodically step back from the system so that we can critically assess how it is operating. The purpose is not to destroy it but to improve on it. We must have the boldness to point out the errors and work to see that they are corrected.

Smith's theory of self-interest has led us to believe that universal prosperity is achieved by seeking personal enrichment. Keynes advised us that economic progress is possible only if we employ the human drive of selfishness.

However, if we allow selfishness and its ambitions to run wild to create wealth, we will also allow greed and envy to run wild. Although the Gross National Product may rise, people will "find themselves oppressed by increasing frustrations, alienation, insecurity, and so forth."[16] Pursuit of self-interest tends to isolate us socially and financially from others. We attempt to become self-reliant instead of reaching out to the fellowship for assistance when adversity comes.

The emphasis on self-interest leads to the single-minded pursuit of wealth as a way to peace and prosperity for all people. Since we believe that we must seek our interests and by doing so we will become wealthy, we believe that the same principle applies to everyone else. We soon find ourselves ignoring the plight of the poor and jobless as we repeat the secular economic wisdom, "a rising tide lifts all boats." The belief is that a rising economy will lift up everybody. Unfortunately, that has not proven to be true. While a rising tide may lift most boats, a rising economy usually also sinks many. The pursuit of self-interest has a hard time dealing with failure and those who may be left behind.

The pursuit of self-interest is also a reason why many of us see work as simply a way to make a living and gain respect or self-respect. Others of us work as a way to accumulate assets. It's not too difficult to see how our system encourages those attitudes.

In capitalism, capital is responsible for the major portion of the wealth produced and labor for only a small fraction of it. Consequently, the distribution of the wealth is done in accordance with the property rights of the persons engaged in production. The worker's attitude shifts from a desire to be good at what he does because that increases his value to a desire to accumulate capital because that is what really increases his value.

Unfortunately, our society hasn't realized that pursuit of self-interest does not create universal prosperity or even individual prosperity. Frequently the opposite occurs. Because our economic system preaches the gospel of self-interest, the inevitable results are stress and despondency when we don't achieve prosperity.

We Christians are without excuse when it comes to pursuing self-interest, yet it's amazing how many persist in adhering to an absolute, self-driven economy. Philippians 2:3, 4 is just as applicable to our economic relationships as it is to our personal ones:

> Do nothing from selfishness or empty conceit, but with humility of mind let each of you regard one another as more important than himself; do not merely look out for your own personal interests, but also for the interests of others.

Mass Consumption

In order to avoid cycles of boom and bust, our economy demands that our consumption of goods and services be maintained at a level to cover constantly increasing levels of production. Marx predicted that the crises caused by these cycles would eventually bring about the collapse of capitalism. Regardless of whether or not he was right, no one wants to experience a blowout of the economy every few years. Avoiding busts is a strong motivation for any kind of economic activity. Consumption has always seemed to be a fairly pleasant and painless way to keep the economy growing. As Keynes has said: "Mass consumption is necessary if all members of a society are to have a high standard of living. What is more significant, mass consumption is necessary to support mass production in an industrial economy."[17] Now we can see where the cult of consumerism was born. It comes from an economic system that requires mass consumption. Without it, we are told, the economy would self-destruct.

To reinforce the notion that consumption is the key to a strong economy, the media inundate us with facts and figures on consumer spending. When consumer outlays fall, we are told that doesn't bode well for the economy. When it rises, economists tell us the economy is growing. The more we spend, the better things will be. The less we spend, the worse things will be. It's our patriotic duty to spend, spend, and spend some more. In return, we are promised a better life, higher standard of living, and freedom from economic depressions.

It could be argued that mass consumption American-style really is necessary to keep the economy growing. However, when we take a look at the capitalism in other countries, we begin to realize that the American way is unhealthy.

The U.S. government always seems to be calling for the West German and Japanese governments to give their consumers "more pocket money, through tax cuts, and to coax them to borrow more through lower interest rates."[18] But that doesn't work. Even if the consumers do get extra money, it's more likely to go into savings than into stores.

In Europe, fear of credit is widespread. "In a study conducted for MasterCard, 45 percent of Europeans in six countries strongly agreed that 'to buy anything other than a house on credit is unwise.' Only 23 percent of Americans responded similarly. And a huge 74 percent of the Europeans surveyed said that credit cards 'make it too easy to overspend,' compared with 21 percent of Americans."[19]

Recently I saw a television ad run by a "credit card repair service." It urged the viewer who couldn't get credit to contact them for help because "Credit is King." Apparently that's true, but it doesn't need to be. We've been made to think that credit is king because it is a powerful tool to stimulate consumption. Yet other capitalist countries have dethroned credit.

Consider Germany where Volkswagen sells half its cars for cash. In America the auto maker sells 95 percent on credit. In 1985 credit accounted for less than 1 percent of Karstadt's (a German department store) $3.1 billion in sales. During that same period Sears, Roebuck & Co. sold 62 percent of its $21.5 billion in volume on credit.

In West Germany, about 70 percent to 85 percent of consumer purchases are paid in cash, according to various estimates; the corresponding figure in the U.S. is about 20 percent. There are only about 1.2 million credit cards in Germany, fewer than in many Third World countries.[20]

In the 1970s Chase Manhattan Corp. established a consumer-finance company with a number of branch offices throughout West Germany. They expected to lend money to German consumers in the same way Americans fell for credit. After a few years the company failed and Chase closed it. A German banker remarked that "they tried to bring the American concept of debt to the German market. It was quite a bloodbath."[21]

Japan offers us another lesson. Although annual per capita income is $300 more than that of the United States, the emphasis in the Japanese economy is definitely not on domestic mass consumption. Even though the Prime Minister has urged the Japanese to spend more and save less, most of the people are not yet convinced that is the thing to do. However, some of the young people are beginning to loosen their grip on their wallets. A walk down the Ginza seems like a walk down Fifth Avenue. But the population as a whole has avoided consumerism.

The habits of other countries show us that mass consumption and the cult of consumerism are not the only ways to live a good life. Our economy will not collapse if we are more prudent in our spending. It's now up to the Christian to challenge an economy of mass consumerism and lead the way to a healthier lifestyle.

The Growth Economy

In order to support the kind of consumption necessary to keep the economy healthy, growth must occur. Our system is one that cannot stand still. Expansion is critical. Protecting our standard of living demands a constant drive to accumulate more, open new markets, and entice the consumer to "move up" to an improved product. The promoters want to cultivate and expand our needs. Yet too few of us realize that this expansion of needs simply increases our dependence on outside forces over which we have no control. The result is greater pressure and stress. We ought to be moving in the opposite direction toward financial freedom. Only by reducing our needs can we reduce so many of the causes of stress.

In economics there has been a tendency toward quantitative analysis rather than qualitative.

For example, having established by his purely quantitative methods that the Gross National Product of a country has risen by, say, five percent, the economist-turned-econometrician is unwilling and generally unable, to face the question of whether this is to be taken as a good thing or a bad thing.[22]

Growth as reflected in the numbers is the primary emphasis of the economist. Consequently, it shouldn't surprise us when the media do little but quote recently released figures and assume that they speak the truth about the economy.

Since the media emphasize the numbers and the quantitative aspects of the economy, so does most of the general public. Growth and expansion become part of our psychological needs. They are assumptions that we make about our lifestyles without questioning.

Four years ago my wife and I bought our first house. It's an older home in an older neighborhood. The price was substantially below both the national and the local average. When we finally decided it was right for us our real estate agent agreed and then added that it was a "perfect starter house." In a few years we would be ready to "move up to something more expensive in a more prestigious neighborhood." The house was (and continues to be) everything we needed. So I asked her why we should move up. Somewhat confused (apparently no one had ever asked that question before), she replied that we would want to — everybody else does.

The move-up syndrome has affected us all, Christian and non-Christian alike. We are told that capitalism is an economy that cannot stand still and have taken that to mean that our personal consumption habits have to keep growing too. The bigger house and the better car are our rights as Americans. Along with that we expect bigger salaries each year. We believe that we must be accumulating more and more wealth. Our bank accounts and savings must grow not necessarily for the real purpose of saving but as another facet of consumerism. With this kind of attitude, financial pressures from a continual emphasis on growth are easily formed.

Production and Advancement

In order for the economy to keep growing, new products and technologies must be continuously introduced. Private enterprise suggests that the totality of life can be reduced to one aspect — profits. The businessman, as a private individual, may still be interested in other aspects of life — perhaps even in goodness, truth, and beauty — but as a businessman he concerns himself only with profits . . . .for private enterprise is not concerned with what it produces but only with what it gains from production.[23]

To gain more, we must produce more. To produce more, we must market more. To market more, we must produce more. It's a vicious cycle. For too many of us, it's a consuming cycle. Our private lives and our charitable activities, even church itself, soon become just other calculated ways to increase our business contacts.

Once again the media pick up on the quantitative aspects. A key indicator of the economy is the rate at which production facilities are used. In recessions, plant operations are usually low. At the peak of an expansion they should be running at full capacity. Thus are we led to an economic value system that demands greater production.

The imperative of production has roots in capitalist theory. Joseph Schumpeter, an eminent conservative economist, has written that

creative destruction is the essential fact about capitalism . . . it is by nature a form or method of economic change, and not only never is, but never can be stationary . . . The fundamental impulse that sets and keeps the capitalist engine in motion comes from the new consumer goods, the new methods of production or transportation, the new markets, the new forms of industrial organization that capitalist enterprise creates.[24]

I am not saying that all new consumer goods are bad or that new methods of production or transportation should be avoided. I am not saying that we should stop striving for new technological advancements or seeking new markets to penetrate. I am not saying that we shouldn't try to improve our present management techniques or forms of industrial organization. But we must realize that the promotion and adoption of every technological advance that will result in a more efficient industrial production of wealth is not always the best course. This especially applies to our individual financial decisions.

We don't have to have a new car just to have a new car. We don't have to buy a new house when an older one will do. We don't have to buy that new TV because it's the product of the latest technical breakthrough. We don't have to fall prey to those consumer product companies whose view of advancement and improvement in the marketplace is to introduce a new toothpaste every month. An advanced product isn't always an enlightened purchase. There is wisdom in sometimes resisting innovation. I don't mean the innovations that are truly needed but those that are made just to add a new wrinkle to an old product. Having the wisdom to see through the innovation that really isn't an innovation will surely prevent needless spending.

Centralization of Wealth

One inevitable consequence of capitalism, whose implication most of us realize but few of us are able to come to grips with, is the centralization of wealth. Will Durant, the widely respected historian, has noted that "the relative equality of Americans before 1776 has been overwhelmed by a thousand forms of physical, mental, and economic differentiation, so that the gap between the wealthiest and the poorest is now greater than at any time since Imperial plutocratic Rome."[25]

Durant wrote this in 1968 before he had a chance to see how the Japanese were aggressively implementing free-market theory. According to *Forbes* magazine, the richest man in America in 1986 was Sam Walton of Wal-Mart. *Forbes* estimated his net worth at $4.5 billion. In October of 1986, a Japanese businessman named Kenji Osano died leaving an estate worth $19 billion.[26] Durant was more right than he knew.

A Congressional Joint Economic Committee Report issued in July 1986 provided some figures on the net worth of Americans: .5 percent of the people have 26.9 percent of the nation's net worth; the next .5 percent have 7.4 percent of the country's net worth; the next 9 percent have 33.6 percent of the net worth. Finally, 90 percent of the people have only 32.1 percent of the nation's net worth.

An analysis of the distribution of trading on the New York Stock Exchange is also revealing. In 1975, 17 percent of all trading on the Exchange was done by institutions. (Institutional

trading refers to blocks of ten thousand or more shares. Typical
institutions include mutual funds, pension funds, banks, life insurance companies, investment companies, and corporations.)
During that same year, 83 percent of trades were by individuals.
In 1986, institutions and individuals both accounted for 50 percent of the trades.[27]

It's not too hard to see why this is happening.

> Because institutions buy and sell huge blocks of stock, they are
> lavished with attention by brokerages. The hundreds of research
> reports written by Wall Street's 2,500 analysts arrive at their doors
> daily, often by messenger. . . . When they do trade, institutions
> buy and sell at deeply discounted commissions — typically 3 to 6
> cents a share. Individuals buying 100 shares of a $50-a-share
> stock pay 78 to 98 cents per share at one big retail brokerage.[28]

The capital market is just one place where we see what could
be considered favor given to the rich. Numerous instances in
dozens of other areas could be pointed out. Yet on careful reflection, what does it mean? On the one hand it seems logical
that large buyers should receive discounts. It seems logical that
big depositors at banks should be treated preferentially. After all,
they are the sources of continued business and profits. But the
little man trying to make ends meet is penalized as a private
player in this large field. No banker greets him at the door when
he walks in to deposit his paycheck. Brokers don't give the one-
time buyer of one hundred shares of General Motors a commission break. It hardly seems fair.

When we take an honest look at our society's treatment of the
rich and the poor in light of Scripture, we are forced to conclude
that something is wrong. Consider Proverbs 22:16:

> He who oppresses the poor to make much for himself or who
> gives to the rich, will only come to poverty.

Isn't that what our society does by favoring the rich? Discrimination like that can only lead to a concentration of wealth.

Our Lord saw that this would happen in a free market. Thus
the reason for the years of remission from debts and the jubilee.
Both were to prevent centralization. Both were to keep the free-
market system in check.

The more freedom in a free market, the greater the concentration of wealth. It is inevitable. We may or may not be able to do anything about it on a governmental level because we must also realize that as economic freedoms decrease, social and political freedoms usually do too. Giving up those will not be an acceptable way to counter centralization of wealth.

Of course, certain governmental changes can and should be made without unduly restricting personal freedoms. But regardless of their effect we all must deal with the issue of concentration of wealth on an individual level. We should recognize that it exists and is a problem that seems to be getting worse. We can see how centralization creates certain financial pressures and attitudes in our own lives, and this awareness should help us deal with the pressures or at least cope with them more effectively.

What Can We Do?

No economic system is inherently right or wrong. The leaders and the way they implement the system will determine how close it comes to being humane.

Every economic system has a tendency to encourage certain behaviors and discourage others. As individuals we usually don't see how the system affects us. It's hard to make a direct connection between economic theory and personal financial decisions. However, the link is definitely there. If we don't acknowledge that link, we will have a tendency to continue in behaviors that are culturally acceptable but not biblically mandated.

As an economic system, capitalism has enabled certain countries to achieve remarkable successes. But those successes shouldn't be allowed to mask the problems that result from such a system. Granted, the problems may not be direct results of the system itself but may have to do with the way individuals take advantage of the way the system operates.

For example, Keynes has said, "For at least another hundred years, we must pretend to ourselves and to everyone that fair is foul and foul is fair; for foul is useful and fair is not. Avarice and usury and precaution [i.e., economic security] must be our gods for a little longer still." Unfortunately, for most of us, avarice and economic security have become gods. We have taken the theory of an economist and made it an object of worship.

Capitalists certainly don't have a corner on greed. But under our system the abuses can be quite spectacular. The stock market's insider trading scandals are good illustrations.

Our assessment of our own personal well-being also reveals much about the way we think. A 1986 article by the respected economist Walter Heller discussed the problems overshadowing our economy. He concluded that, in spite of the problems, we have great economic strengths to draw on. Our two greatest strengths are that "we have the highest per-capita wealth of any industrial nation" and "in terms of per-capita consumption, our standard [of living] is also still the highest in the industrial world."[29]

That's how economists judge us — by our wealth and our standard of living. The way the experts look at us has also become the way we judge ourselves. Our bank accounts and our lifestyles are extremely important to us. They give us value and status as individuals. Yet we have accepted economic criteria as correct without raising a biblical standard in comparison. God does not judge us by our wealth or standard of living.

Making judgments based on wealth eventually leads to isolation from the poor and indifference toward them. Consider the California town where residents have sought to overturn a ruling that allows overnight sleeping in vacant public lots. In that same town a shopkeeper once doused discarded food with bleach to keep the hungry from "dumpster-diving." In a New Jersey town, officials have likened building a shelter to posting a "neon light" inviting vagrants from nearby cities. In Chicago, complaints by joggers and picnickers led officials to demand that a homeless man leave.[30] In Dallas, more than five hundred people came to a hearing to protest proposed sites for public housing. No one wanted the poor or minority groups living in their neighborhoods. I could go on and on with such examples.

It is becoming apparent that there are some things capitalism does not do well. Providing adequate health care and establishing housing for all are clear examples. The dramatic rise in the number of homeless has finally begun to receive media attention. There has been an alarming jump in the poverty rate in the 1980s. "The number of people in poverty has risen by one-third since 1979."[31] Unless we acknowledge these kinds of problems instead of blindly accepting the kind of economic system touted by our political leaders, the financial pressures on all of us will become even greater burdens.

Of course there are always problems with any system. However, our responsibility as Christians must be to recognize those created by our own system. We should realize the emphasis put on self-interest, accumulation of wealth, consumption, growth, production, and new products. We must acknowledge that our present system leads to a centralization of the wealth. Knowing the relationship between these results, economic theory, and our own actions will give us a greater insight into where some of our financial pressures come from.

Step #5 to Financial Freedom

Be aware of what the prevailing economic theories are and how they influence individual financial decisions.

SIX

WHATEVER HAPPENED TO INTEGRITY?

Values

Robert Harley, the Earl of Oxford, founded the South Sea Company in 1711. Although his company wasn't destined to last long, it would serve as a tremendous embarrassment and path to bankruptcy for thousands of Englishmen. To us it will be a reminder that the strongest of values can easily be forgotten.

The Earl's new company invited the holders of 9 million pounds of government bonds to exchange their bonds for stock in the South Sea Company. In return for this patriotic service in retiring part of the national debt, the Crown granted a monopoly on English trade with South America and the South Sea islands to the South Sea Company. Harley hoped that precious metals from the New World would make him and the stockholders fabulously wealthy.

Unfortunately, the monopoly wasn't all it was cracked up to be. The Earl had neglected to account for one minor variable — Spain, the ruler of most of South America at the time. Spain was unwilling to open its colonies to more than just a token amount of British trade. But Harley was not discouraged. He was more than able to spin an enticing story to a greedy and gullible public. So in 1720, the South Sea Company made Parliament an offer that couldn't be ignored. Harley asked Parliament to issue South Sea stock to England's bondholders. In return the company would absorb virtually the entire national debt of 31 million pounds.

To support his case, the Earl and his allies cranked up the rumor mill. They whispered that England and Spain were negotiating treaties that would give England free trade with all of the Spanish colonies. Gold and silver would flood England from the New World. The South Sea merchants and investors would become the richest on earth. Stockholders would receive hundreds of pounds annually for every hundred they invested.

In the face of these claims there were few dissenters. But Robert Walpole was one. He would later become Britain's first Prime Minister. In the House of Commons he denounced the plan, saying it was designed "to raise artificially the value of the stock, by exciting and keeping up a general infatuation, and by promising dividends out of funds which could never be adequate to the purpose."[1] Walpole's eloquence was not persuasive. The bill passed.

The speculation was intense. In January 1720, the price was 128½ pounds per share. By August, it had soared to 1,000 pounds per share. All kinds of people joined the mad rush to buy stock. "It seemed at times as if the whole nation had turned stock-jobbers [traders]. Exchange Alley was every day blocked up by crowds, and Cornhill [a street in London's financial district] was impassable for the number of carriages. Everybody came to purchase stock."[2]

It wasn't long before swindlers formed hundreds of "bubble companies" to take advantage of the market conditions. These companies had no purpose other than to raise money for their promoters. One was organized "for trading in hair." Another tried to raise 1 million pounds to manufacture a perpetual-motion machine. And another was set up "for the transmutation of quicksilver [mercury] into a malleable fine metal"—an interesting prospect since mercury is liquid at any temperature above minus-38 degrees Fahrenheit.

Remarkably, one company was established with no stated purpose at all. The prospectus said the company was organized "for carrying on an undertaking of great advantage, but nobody is to know what it is." The promoter told subscribers that for every 2 pounds invested they would receive 100 pounds in dividends. A 50 to 1 return was hard to resist. A crowd of people appeared at this man's door the morning after the prospectus was published. He raised 2,000 pounds in six hours. Satisfied with his day's work, this particular entrepreneur "was philosopher enough to be contented with his venture, and set off the same evening for the Continent. He was never heard of again."[3]

In August of 1720 the South Sea Bubble burst. News leaked out that the directors of the company, including the chairman, had sold their stock. This triggered massive panic selling. The price of the stock dove from 1,000 pounds to only 135 pounds. Thousands of families were devastated, and a general depression hit England.

Christian Convictions or Convictions of the Masses?

Like the Dutch tulip mania, certain economic practices, especially those in the banking industry, made the South Sea Bubble possible. But expansion of credit is not the point of this story. Instead our focus is on how money and the pressures of the crowd can suddenly change our values. Listen to Charles Mackay describe what happened:

> Men were no longer satisfied with the slow but sure profits of cautious industry. The hope of boundless wealth for the morrow made them heedless and extravagant for today. A luxury, till then unheard of, was introduced, bringing in its train a corresponding laxity of morals. The overbearing insolence of ignorant men, who had arisen to sudden wealth by successful gambling, made men of true gentility of mind and manners blush that gold should have power to raise the unworthy in the scale of society.[4]

How could so many men of integrity, stature, and discipline turn from their convictions so rapidly? The events of the day and the social pressure of so many people going in one direction blinded many to the truth of their own values. The crowd was just too strong.

Like those men who lost heavily in the Bubble, we are seduced and misled by the crowd every day. The circumstances are usually not as obvious as those of the South Sea Bubble. But the subtlety of these issues shouldn't mask their importance. Their effect on us can be remarkable. Mass opinion and mass acceptance of certain values can lead us to do things that we could not conceive of in our more thoughtful moments. The convictions of the crowd can easily replace the convictions we should have as Christians.

The Place of Money

In 1986, UCLA's Higher Education Research Institute and the American Council on Education surveyed 280,000 college freshmen on 550 campuses. Of that group, 71 percent said "being very well off financially" was their goal. Nineteen years ago 83 percent named "developing a meaningful philosophy of life" as their goal. About 25 percent now want a business career. Fewer than 1 percent will be English majors — down 80 percent since the 1967 survey.[5]

Where do our college freshman get these kinds of values? For many it's the prospect of large starting salaries at major corporations, law firms, or accounting firms. Others may flock to "New York brokerage houses, investment banks and financial law firms. Nowhere else in America can someone barely out of college earn a six-figure salary so soon." One Wall Street lawyer observed that "they want to feel rich and powerful. It's a game they play to feel the adrenalin flow."[6]

Ivan Boesky was one Wall Street deal maker who couldn't stay on top. He paid $100 million to settle charges by the Securities and Exchange Commission that he had used inside information to profit on takeover bids. In spite of the publicity surrounding Boesky and other SEC targets, the use of insider information is still not seen as an abuse of ethical standards by some. One Wall Street broker asked, "Isn't everyone doing it?" He also compared rules against insider trading with the old 55-mile-per-hour speed limit — a law that everyone paid lip service to, but few obeyed.[7]

The insider trading scandal was one of the more publicized acts of our money-oriented culture. As we move down the income ladder the publicity may decrease, but the emphasis on money doesn't. Clearly, the attitude toward money in our society is that it is something with intrinsic value — to be desired because of the pleasure, security, status, and power it gives us. This is the social reality of money in contemporary Western cultures. To our condemnation as believers, most of us have accepted that reality as part of our own value system.

There is very little difference between the lifestyle of a typical Protestant evangelical and that of his non-Christian counterpart.

Their houses look the same, their cars are the same, their clothes are the same, and their furniture is the same. That's not necessarily wrong. However, the outward similarities are too often signs of the inward similarities.

Even though we are Christians, our greatest desires are no different from those of our peers — upward mobility and financial independence. Those particular goals are the stars we steer by. They set our direction and we are always pointing toward them. At church we are more comfortable talking about our jobs and investments than our spiritual growth. When a friend asks how we are doing the natural tendency is for the conversation to head toward some part of our secular lives — work, sports, or whatever has captured the most media attention that week. Prayer, faith, spiritual growth, the majesty of God, and saving the lost never quite rate high enough. Sometimes it's hard to tell whether a believer really does operate under a different value system.

What we cling to on the outside is a symbol of our inner attitude. Jesus made this clear: "For where your treasure is, there will your heart be also" (Luke 12:34). It's true that money buys a certain degree of pleasure, security, status, and power. Only the naive would deny that. The point is not whether money can buy those things but whether it is right to seek them. Scripture says it is not right. The believer must operate under a different value system from the world's.

To live by that system will require a different attitude about life and about money. Further, it's not enough to say we'll change our attitudes but keep living like the world. Too few believers have successfully done that. A changed value system requires a change in the way we handle the trappings of money. It requires us to be different outwardly.

The Meaning of Possessions

In keeping with our money-centered value system, we acquire possessions. They tell us that our value system is all right, and because we perceive our possessions as responses to our needs, we don't have to think very hard about the rightness or wrongness of buying them. We need something, so why not buy it?

The missing link in our decision-making process has been the unwillingness to question what we see as "needs." When we think that we need a new car or new clothes, we rarely stop to consider where that need comes from. Is it because we really need it or because of outside influences like peers or advertising? Have we considered the alternatives to purchasing the items?

We should be careful when we consider a need. Schumacher in *Small Is Beautiful* had some interesting comments on needs.

> The cultivation and expansion of needs is the antithesis of wisdom. It is also the antithesis of freedom and peace. Every increase of needs tends to increase one's dependence on outside forces over which one cannot control, and therefore increases existential fear. Only by a reduction of needs can one promote a genuine reduction in those tensions which are the ultimate causes of strife and war.[8]

Whether we agree with Schumacher's economics or not, his point is well taken. The more we need, the more bound we are by those needs. Eventually, the needs become so important that we are driven to meet them by whatever means necessary. On a national level that could mean war. On an individual level all we have to do is look at the drug addicts. They are liable to do anything for a fix. Bringing the analogy closer to home—what are we willing to do to maintain our lifestyles? Take any job, slant the truth, let others go hungry? Our needs control our money habits.

A Biblical Model

Let's go one step further back. Needs determine what we spend our dollars on. But where do needs come from? Needs ultimately derive from our values.[9] If we value a comfortable and luxurious lifestyle, then we will "need" certain accoutrements to support that lifestyle. If we value individualism, as our society does, then we will tend to hold on to our possessions more tightly. We will fear losing them and what others might do to them.

Consequently, we conveniently overlook certain biblical passages that would have a freeing effect on us if we applied them. One of them is Acts 4:32,34,35:

> And the congregation of those who believed were of one heart and soul; and not one of them claimed that anything belonging to him was his own; but all things were common property to

them. . . . For there was not a needy person among them, for all who were owners of land or houses would sell them and bring the proceeds of the sales, and lay them at the apostles' feet; and they would be distributed to each, as any had need.

This was not necessarily a mandate for common ownership. However, it is showing us the freedom we should have as believers in regard to our possessions. On the one hand, there should be no need for fear and wondering how our legitimate needs will be met. On the other hand, false "needs" should not be cultivated.

Our individualism and our fear of socialism have led us to ignore what went on in the early church. Whether there was any connection between what they did and verse thirty-three ("And with great power the apostles were giving witness to the resurrection of the Lord Jesus, and abundant grace was upon them all") is hard to tell. But it is clear that their focus was taken off possessions and put on the true calling of the church. At the very least this freed them up to concentrate on their role as witnesses to a lost world instead of on how they might acquire more property and live a better lifestyle. We might be able to learn something from our early church ancestors after all. Perhaps if we shifted our values from the pursuit of the American lifestyle, we might be more successful at advancing the Kingdom of God in our society.

The Media's Effect on Values

We've already seen some of the ways most people in our society pick up their money values—economics and advertising are two of the obvious ones. Of course, the fallenness of man's nature is also a contributor. But another interesting, alarming, and potentially very dangerous way that values are communicated is the communication medium itself.

Printed materials are no more threatening than they have always been. However, television has become a special phenomenon. The events and the people we see on the screen have become more real than their counterparts in real life. For example, at a recent law school graduation, the commencement speaker was someone who played a judge on television. A TV doctor who made a commercial for a medication had this opening line:

"I'm not a doctor, but I play one on TV." Should we believe him instead of a real doctor?

The 1987 World Almanac Heroes of Young America poll asked high-school students who their heroes were. The top ten were: Bill Cosby, Sylvester Stallone, Eddie Murphy, Ronald Reagan, Chuck Norris, Clint Eastwood, Molly Ringwald, Rob Lowe, Arnold Schwarzenegger, and Don Johnson. With the exception of Ronald Reagan (who once *was* an actor) they all are actors. "Celebrity counts for everything. If you are famous, you are a hero. If you are not famous, you are nothing."[10] The value is in the actor or the character he plays. Reality doesn't matter.

The danger is that our society may soon come to hold a value system even more unreal than the one we have now. It will be a value system created totally out of thin air with no moral or ethical foundation. And unless we are careful, Christians will be sucked right in—just like before.

Security

Perhaps the most potentially damaging value that we Christians have imitated is reflected in our perceived need for security. We want the security afforded by steady jobs, air-tight insurance policies, and a government that will take care of us if we fall on hard times. We want to feel secure in our own homes and then just be left alone. In return, we won't bother anybody else. Of course, that also means we won't bother them with our faith either.

Francis Schaeffer calls this value "personal peace." The majority of people came to it through "art, music, drama, theology, and the mass media." It has now gone beyond merely an accepted viewpoint to "an almost monolithic consensus."[11] Schaeffer defines it as follows: "Personal peace means just to be left alone, not to be troubled by the troubles of other people, whether across the world or across the city—to live one's life with minimal possibilities of being personally disturbed. Personal peace means wanting to have my personal life pattern undisturbed in my lifetime, regardless of what the result will be in the lifetime of my children and grandchildren."[12]

Since personal peace and security are such strong motivators there has been a tendency to embrace certain economic principles that would promote those values. The result of these values and principles working in concert can be seen on a number of different levels.

First, we have allowed the government (especially federal) to grow strong and powerful. It penetrates every segment of our society, and we now see it as our salvation in time of need. Government has become our god, and its agencies are the churches where we worship. But ultimately government is not capable of acting as a god. In certain areas and at certain times it will not be able to perform. We see this in little ways today. Benefits are denied for some illogical reason, funds run out and programs can't be renewed, a regulation forces a legitimate and worthy business to shut down or keeps another one from starting—all show the frequent ineptitude of government. Yet we continue to believe in its power, and when it fails, we are so disillusioned that the resulting pressure is hard to deal with.

Right now these are all minor examples. But the day will come when a catastrophe will strike and our government will be powerless. Perhaps this will be through another depression. Regardless, if we continue to rely on government as a god, the financial pressures created by its inability to perform in a crisis may be too much to bear.

We have also put our trust in large corporations. There is security in size. Temporarily, working for a large corporation can relieve pressures. The pay may be good and the job itself secure. The prospect of a reliable pension is comforting, and knowing that you've got a great health insurance plan helps you sleep much better. As the Japanese say: "Everybody wants to be under a big tree so they can be protected when a storm hits."

All these things are wonderful, but a large company isn't immune to an economic slump either. Layoffs can happen. Bankruptcies are no longer uncommon. Reliance on the company can create tremendous financial pressures when it no longer runs smoothly.

Then there are the insurance companies. We are so unsure of ourselves and so fearful of loss that our society can't function without insurance. Either we want insurance or somebody requires us to have insurance for every conceivable risk. This is not to say that we should go out and cancel all our insurance policies. But we must realize that our security is not with an insurance company.

Moral Hazards or Moral Behavior?

As we strive for more and more security at all levels of our society, a curious thing begins to happen. George Gilder describes this in *Wealth and Poverty:*

> In the delicate balance between the risk and insurance features of capitalism, the boundaries are defined by what insurance companies term "moral hazard." Moral hazard is the danger that a policy will encourage the behavior—or promote the disasters—that it insures against.[13]

For example, an arsonist may not have second thoughts about burning a building because he knows the owner is protected. Even worse, an owner may burn his own building to collect the insurance proceeds. Health insurance may have a tendency to raise medical costs. In certain situations welfare benefits may keep someone from working.

In many instances,

> a pressure is exerted on behalf of the behavior insured against and a penalty is inflicted on the behavior that the insurer desires. People with good health habits pay for the smokers, drinkers, and drug abusers, the neurotic propagators of venereal disease, the reckless drivers, the over-eaters, the under-sleepers, the slothful and improvident, as well as for the maligners and the entrepreneurial pursuers of disability claims.[14]

The solution is to take our trust off the illusory security provided by insurers, corporations, and government. Gilder goes on to show how the results of moral hazards were less likely under the informal, familial, and church aid that preceded mass insurance. Those groups exerted strong moral pressures in favor of preferred behaviors. "In Oriental communities in America these disciplines have worked so well that even in the midst of the Great Depression, only a handful of Chinese and Japanese sought government aid."[15]

Perhaps there was something to what the early Christians did after all. At least they recognized that their security was not in some human institution but in God and His sovereignty. That sovereignty was frequently seen through the church and a fellowship of believers who took care of one another so that financial pressures wouldn't immobilize the members. They were not so individualistic that the values of personal peace and security ruled their lives.

The Importance of Work

We've already seen how work or a job has become an end in itself. The natural consequence is that our job becomes everything to us. It's not only where we work but where we play, give, and worship.

The job, or the company, becomes so important that our lives must be oriented around it. Where we play and what we play at are determined by the workplace. Some companies have even institutionalized the play through athletic leagues and facilities.

The rise of corporate giving efforts has been interesting. It wasn't too long ago that the United Way was just another group of charitable organizations with a fairly low-keyed funding effort. But somehow it was taken on as the beneficiary of corporate America. Over the years some corporations have developed such an intense effort to persuade their employees to give that they could be called nothing less than "strong-arm tactics." One major company told its employees that if they didn't give their "fair share" (a certain percentage of their income), they would be required to go on a tour of United Way agencies in their town! A friend of mine refused to give, and he was indeed loaded on a bus for the tour. After the tour, he was pressured again, but to his credit he didn't give in. There are many good organizations in the United Way, but companies should not try to shame an employee into giving.

Most corporate largess is directed at the arts. Funding for the arts has typically been a relatively noncontroversial subject. Everybody wants to support the arts, and with so many struggling artists around, there is even a touch of relief work to the gifts. However, corporate emphasis on arts funding to the exclusion or at the expense of other causes can only be compared to an act of worship. Art is the religion of American corporations. Its parishioners are corporate patrons and its tithe the corporate grant. There are many worthy recipients in the arts, but none worthy of the kind of worship bestowed on them by corporations.

On the surface our society appears somewhat schizophrenic. Corporate executives give to the arts, but they also perceive work as an end rather than a means. The latter view is expressed "by the way we subordinate to economic activity the much more important and difficult creative activities that lie outside the sphere of the production of wealth—the activities of politics, religion, the fine arts, pure science, philosophy, teaching, etc."[16]

Although our value system still puts a premium on work, we have a conscience that makes us feel like we ought to be giving to something. There are just enough remnants of an old value system that put a priority on giving and supporting worthy endeavors to make us feel guilty if we don't give. Thus the tension between encouraging economic activity and giving to the arts. This will probably not last. As financial pressures build in corporations, giving to the arts will decline. There is no solid value system to support it.

One value that will last longer is credentialism. As Gilder has written, it is

characterized by a worship of degrees, diplomas, tests, credentials, and qualifications [and] has created a schoolmarm meritocracy that steadily extends the reach of its primary rule: you cannot pass if you cannot parse; if you cannot put the numbers in the right boxes at the requisite speed; and if you cannot perform in the accustomed academic mode.[17]

Credentialism has created untold financial pressures for hundreds of thousands, perhaps millions, of people. The worship of credentials will affect the type of first job you are given, whether or not you will be promoted, when you get a raise, what type of assignment you are given, and whether or not you are to be terminated. We are told that credentialism is an objective way to make a decision about an employee. But in truth it is no more than an integral part of a value system that glorifies work for work's sake.

Creativity in the Workplace Only

As work has become more and more important to society, we Christians have increasingly melted into our own work. We are now just as good as the next person at thinking up creative solutions to problems we face on the job. We spend just as much overtime as the next fellow developing innovative approaches and new techniques that will produce greater profit. Yet we have neglected doing the same thing with our spiritual lives.

Jesus told a parable that speaks to this condition. It's found in Luke 16:1-13:

> There was a certain rich man who had a steward, and this steward was reported to him as squandering his possessions. And he called him and said to him, "What is this I hear about you? Give an account of your stewardship, for you can no longer be steward." And the steward said to himself, "What shall I do, since my master is taking the stewardship away from me? I am not strong enough to dig; I am ashamed to beg. I know what I shall do, so that when I am removed from the stewardship, they will receive me into their homes." And he summoned each one of his master's debtors, and he began saying to the first, "How much do you owe my master?" And he said "A hundred measures of oil." And he said to him, "Take your bill, and sit down quickly and write fifty." Then he said to another, "And how much do you owe?" And he said, "A hundred measures of wheat." He said to him, "Take your bill and write eighty." And his master praised the unrighteous steward because he had acted shrewdly; for the sons of this age are more shrewd in relation to their own kind than the sons of light. And I say to you, make friends for yourselves by means of the mammon of unrighteousness; that when it fails, they may receive you into the eternal dwellings. He who is faithful in a very little thing is faithful also in much; and he who is unrighteous in a very little thing is unrighteous also in much. If therefore you have not been faithful in the use of unrighteous mammon, who will entrust the true riches to you? And if you have not been faithful in the use of that which is another's, who will give you that which is your own? No servant can serve two masters; for either he will hate the one, and love the other, or else he will hold to one, and despise the other. You cannot serve God and mammon.

An interesting television commercial was produced recently by a computer giant. It showed a good-looking man driving down a deserted road in his foreign sports car. All of a sudden he stops and turns the car around. He goes back to what looks like the "last-chance" gas station and rushes to the pay phone. He is calling corporate headquarters to let them know that he has just come up with the solution to his client's problem.

The inference, of course, is that this company's employees are always working for the client — even when they are on vacation. They are always thinking of innovative answers to problems. They are acting shrewdly for their client.

The sons of this age are more shrewd than the sons of light. Their primary motivation in life is work, and they spare no expense, effort, or time in developing clever techniques to increase profit. But the sons of light should be a different story. Our primary motivation is to glorify God and witness to the world. How much effort do we put into that? How shrewd are we when it comes to developing new techniques to reach the lost, in coming up with creative answers to problems faced by our local church, or in developing innovative solutions for overcoming barriers to spreading the Gospel? We are shrewd at work, but when it comes to our Christian commitment, we seem to have left our cleverness at the office.

That's because our values are at the office too. It's not church that excites us to be creative; it's the prospect of profit. Our wisdom is mainly used on selfish or secular goals instead of godly ones. Like the steward, we are shrewd and wise at work, but not in those things that really matter in the eyes of God. The steward's "cleverness is not an isolated phenomenon: it is part of the way of the world. The worldlings show far more *savoir faire* than the religious in dealing with the contemporaries. For even their roguery is often designed to procure them friends, while the pious too often estrange those who might be friendly to them."[18]

The shrewdness and dedication of most Christians pale in comparison to those committed to other causes. Consider the socialists.

> Several times a week, the 25 to 30 Dallas area members of the Socialist Workers Party and the Young Socialist Alliance gather to sit on the folding chairs lined up in the . . . back room. They discuss, explain and protest the world's injustices and violence. . . . On Saturday mornings, the socialists make forays into the streets or malls to sell *The Militant, Young Socialist, and Perspectiva Mindial.* During the week, they may stand outside the gates of industrial plants or vie with the downtown street preachers for the attention of the crowds waiting for buses.[19]

The Muslims have a group named Tablighi Jamaat, or the "preaching association." One of their primary purposes is to propagate the Muslim faith around the world. "As a self-supporting lay movement, members insist on paying their own way and will not even accept a free cup of tea. They contribute one month of their time each year to attend conventions and to go out with teams on preaching tours."[20]

The communists didn't just march into Afghanistan one day without some advance notice. Years ago students from Russia went to study at the University of Kabul. They didn't go for its academics, but because of their missionary zeal. "It was not long before most of the students at Kabul University openly declared themselves to be Communists."[21]

While other dedicated groups have put their values in front of their society's, we Christians have left our shrewdness and creativity in the workplace. As part of our justification we have ignored or misinterpreted the main point of the parable of the unrighteous steward.

We've interpreted the parable financially. We've taken the words, "He who is faithful in a very little thing is faithful also in much" and "If therefore you have not been faithful in the use of unrighteous mammon, who will entrust the true riches to you?" and turned them into directives to invest and make huge profits. These words refer to how we acquire and use worldly goods, which in reality are the "little things" with the smallest intrinsic value. The verses do not mean that good investment management of small amounts will bring larger ones.

Although the steward was unrighteous, we are not to be like him in that respect. His shrewdness may be admired and his application of that within his value system can be a lesson to us. But our value system should cause us to be free from the low motives that dominated him. We should use our goods and intellect for God in a manner that will glorify Him and bring blessings to others. We should be free from avarice and the desire to make the accumulation and enjoyment of material goods the main object of our lives. To do otherwise is to value our work for the wrong reasons.

Our Fragile Lives

Many of us realize that our values have been wrong only when it's too late. At that point we come to grips with our mortality and suddenly wonder what we've done with our lives. Scripture tries to warn us and awaken us before it's too late. In Ecclesiastes 12:1-7 we are made to face the fact of our mortality through one of the most awesome sequences of word-pictures in the Bible:

> Remember also your Creator in the days of your youth, before the evil days come and the years draw near when you will say, "I have no delight in them"; before the sun, the light, the moon, and the stars are darkened, and clouds return after the rain; in the day that the watchmen of the house tremble, and mighty men stoop, the grinding ones stand idle because they are few, and those who look through windows grow dim; and the doors on the street are shut as the sound of the grinding mill is low, and one will arise at the sound of the bird, and all the daughters of song will sing softly. Furthermore, men are afraid of a high place and of terrors on the road; the almond tree blossoms, the grasshopper drags himself along, and the caperberry is ineffective. For man goes to his eternal home while mourners go about in the street. Remember Him before the silver cord is broken and the golden bowl is crushed, the pitcher by the well is shattered and the wheel at the cistern is crushed; then the dust will return to the earth as it was, and the spirit will return to God who gave it.

In verse two we see a picture of gloom and darkness, not unlike the fading physical and mental powers brought on by old age. Other lights are withdrawn — old friends, familiar customs, long-held hopes. In youth there is always the prospect of recovery of these. Troubles and illnesses are just setbacks. In old age they are disasters. Consequently, we must confront these facts in youth when we can be moved to action, not in age when we are moved to despair and regrets.

Verse three reveals more signs of age — trembling watchmen, stooping mighty men, idle grinders, and dim eyes. Then in verse four the image is of hearing loss. No longer can the grinding in the mill or the chirping of birds be heard.

We observe an old man's fear of falling in verse five and see his white hair in the image of the almond tree blossoms. The sight of a grasshopper dragging himself along parodies the quickness of youth. Even desire itself fails of which the caper-berry is emblematic—it was "highly regarded as a stimulus to appetite and an aphrodisiac."[22]

Verse six shows us both the beauty and the fragility of our human body. We are like a golden bowl suspended by a fine silver cord. Suddenly the cord snaps, and the bowl drops to the floor, shattering like a piece of pottery. We are then as useless as a broken wheel. Finally, death claims us, and our spirit returns to its Maker.

Our mortality is undeniable, yet too few of us have adopted a value system that shows we know that. We spend our most creative energies and our most valuable time on work and accumulating wealth. To most of us, "retirement" means that the task of providing enough wealth for economic security is completed and the main purpose of life has been accomplished.

Our values must be shifted. We are called to acknowledge our mortality early in life. Granted, it's never too late to be used by the Lord, but those who know what to do in youth and deny it until they are financially secure are committing a grave error.

God doesn't want us to work away our most productive years in order to build an estate to live off in the later years. He wants us to work for Him *now*. We are mortal. We may not have the opportunity to live off our accumulated wealth. We may not be able to work for Him when we retire. "Death has not yet reached out to us: let it rattle its chains at us and stir us into action!"[23]

The Emphasis on Success

Once we grapple with the idea of our mortality and finally realize where we are in the grand scheme of history, it's time to stand toe-to-toe with what may very well be the most outrageous, deceptive, and destructive theology in modern Christendom. Maybe those words are too harsh, but I think not. When it comes to the gospel of success, I can only say: "We've been duped!"

Hardly a day goes by when I'm not told by someone that God wants me to be successful. It comes in many forms. A radio preacher promises that God wants me to be rich. A television preacher says God will bless me—material blessing is firmly implied—beyond my wildest dreams. A few years ago I was in the audience of a preacher who is now very well known internationally and wrote down this part of his sermon: "An obedient believer cannot be a loser—they are always successful."

Then there are the positive-thinking pundits of the pulpit. They tell us that right thinking, right programming, right motivation and right techniques will turn our failures into glorious successes. They *say* that faith turns losers into winners, yet what they really mean is that confidence in our own potential turns losers into winners. After all, Jesus Himself said seek God's Kingdom first and *everything* will be added to us.

Our prophets then get practical. Why drive a ten-year-old Chevy when you ought to own a classy new Mercedes-Benz? Why live in that old $70,000 house when you ought to buy a new $170,000 home? Even our pastors are exhorted to get in step. Why lead a 100-person congregation when you ought to have 3,000 and a dynamic television ministry?

At least we don't *worship* success like the rest of the world. Right? But, how different really are our values from those of Andrew Carnegie, the steel tycoon, who said, "I would not give a fig for the young man who does not already see himself the partner or the head of an important firm. Do not rest content for a moment in your thoughts as head clerk, or foreman, or general manager in any concern, no matter how extensive. Say to yourself, 'My place is at the top' "?[24]

Success has even been institutionalized. In his study, *The Gospel According to the Harvard Business School,* Peter Kohen noted that the apparent value system taught at Harvard is "the American way . . . which urges people to compete for the sake of competing, win for the sake of winning, and which honors him who does all of this without pause or let-up—the fastest, the nicest, the sportiest, the artiest; because things wouldn't be the way they are unless God meant them to be."[25]

Survival of the Wealthiest

How did we get to be this way? First, it must be acknowledged that this kind of success theology is not new. That's clear from Hosea 12:8: "And Ephraim said, 'Surely I have become rich, I have found wealth for myself; in all my labors they will find in me no iniquity, which would be sin.'" As far back as the time of Hosea there was a tendency to equate the presence of wealth with the absence of sin. But that kind of thinking wouldn't account for the popularity of the success gospel today.

There is one possible explanation for its origin. Absolute proof is not possible, but the theory is intriguing.

Herbert Spencer (1820-1903) was an English philosopher and sociologist. Contrary to popular belief, it is to Spencer that we owe the phrase "survival of the fittest." He took Charles Darwin's theory of natural selection and transferred it from biology to economic and social life. Spencer did give a great deal of credit to Darwin, though:

> I am simply carrying out the views of Mr. Darwin in their applications to the human race . . . all [members of the race] being subject to the "increasing difficulty of getting a living . . ." there is an average advance under the pressure, since only those who do advance under it eventually survive; and . . . these must be the select of their generation.[26]

Spencer wrote numerous books. In England they were influential, "but in the United States they were very little less than divine revelation."[27] His books sold rapidly and widely, and they were greeted with great enthusiasm. Now no one needed to feel guilty over having wealth. It was the inevitable result of natural selection. The rich were superior—the fittest who had survived.

It wasn't long before Spencer began to attract American disciples. One was a Yale professor named William Graham Sumner. His case for the rich is as follows:

> The millionaires are a product of natural selection . . . It is because they are thus selected that wealth—both their own and that entrusted to them—aggregates under their hands . . . They may fairly be regarded as the naturally selected agents of society for certain work. They get high wages and live in luxury, but the bargain is a good one for society.[28]

A corollary to Spencer's theory is that by natural selection the poor must be weeded out. Therefore, the Christian can logically extend the theory to say that since the rich are selected to survive and since God has selected us as His children, He must intend for us to be rich.

The irony of it all is the thought that today's version of the success gospel may very well be a product of, or at least reinforced by, Spencer's theories. It's ironic because those who so strongly assail the theory of evolution on a biological level have accepted it on an economic level. If biological natural selection is contrary to Scriptural truth, then surely economic natural selection is as well.

Of course the thought that the rich are better has always existed. Evolution and Spencer's theories just legitimized it. Once it was legitimized, Social Darwinism (as it was then known) began to fade. Now we have taken a different approach by putting money in the place of long-held democratic ideals. For example, we have turned the "pursuit of happiness" into the pursuit of wealth.

> We regard wealth as if it were a good without qualification or without limit — the more of it the better, no matter how it is used. We forget that the acquisition of wealth by a household is only a means to an end. . . . We, therefore, fail to recognize that the amount of wealth that any household needs is strictly limited, and that the amount in excess of reasonable needs which it can put to good use is relatively slight.[29]

Our culture has given the pursuit of wealth an intrinsic value. Getting rich at any cost is fine: it is the American way.

Consider a man profiled by *Forbes* magazine some time ago. This person plays "white knight" for big publicly traded companies. Canadian-based Campeau Corporation wanted to take over Allied Stores. They made an offer to buy Allied. But Allied didn't want to be bought by Campeau. So Allied asked this man and his backers to make a second offer. He would be the "white knight" who would rescue Allied. But suddenly Campeau dropped their offer and announced they had purchased 48 percent of Allied from a Los Angeles-based brokerage house. This "white knight" and his group were so upset that they filed suit against both Campeau and the brokerage. In the end they pocketed as a settlement $53 million, plus $65 million for expenses.

This man boasts about losing that offer plus two others. And why not? — he made millions for himself and his investors. By targeting victims for somebody else's takeover, he wins lucrative "consolation prizes." As *Forbes* concluded:

> A sad commentary that a man can get rich extracting money from public companies, get backing from a major investment house for doing so and feel free to boast about his high-stakes gamesmanship.[30]

Nobody said the pursuit of wealth by the naturally selected was supposed to be ethical.

No Room for Failure

With so much emphasis on wealth and success in our society, how is failure treated? Frankly, there seems to be a paranoid aversion to discussing failure or admitting it. We don't even want to mention the word. "Error" or "mistake" would be more appropriate.

In spite of the fact that failure is much more common than success, the study of failure is virtually ignored in university curricula. Some academics are trying to change that, yet they also realize that success sells and failure doesn't. The same is true in consulting, in books, and at conferences and seminars.

Thomas Peters, co-author of the best-seller *In Search of Excellence*, acknowledges that failure is not discussed in business circles.

> There's still a prevailing frontier optimism . . . So we don't talk about failure, we don't write about it, we don't even think about it. . . . [Consultants] get paid better when they say optimistic things. . . . The response of the market to books with titles like mine shows you where the interest is.[31]

The depth of our fear of failure can be seen in the way we treat bad news. When Sun Oil lays off employees, it is "only managing . . . staff resources. Sometimes you manage them up and sometimes you manage them down."[32]

Herbalife International, Inc. recently paid $850,000 to "settle charges by authorities that it made false claims in promoting its nutritional and weight-loss products, and agreed to change some of the claims."³³ You would think that would be an embarrassment hard to avoid. But the President of the company saw it in a different light. He said in a press release:

> Today represents a milestone for Herbalife — a solid foundation that is built on the confidence given to us today by statements issued by state and federal regulatory agencies. I am pleased to announce that, after more than a year and a half of discussions and negotiations with the Food and Drug Administration, the California State Attorney General and the California Department of Health, all three agencies have independently determined that Herbalife products have been and still are safe for the American public. Furthermore, all of our product claims, labeling and marketing materials are now in conformance with the spirit and the letter of both federal and state law.³⁴

That's quite a mouthful for explaining an $850,000 penalty. You would think the government was giving the company a medal of honor instead of a fine for unethical conduct.

Using verbosity and doublespeak to mask failure is widespread. *The Quarterly Review of Doublespeak,* published by the National Council of Teachers of English, has collected numerous examples. One recent Doublespeak Award went to the description of the Three Mile Island debacle. Public relations people described fire as "rapid oxidation" and an explosion as "energetic disassembly." The damaged reactor core was releasing no more heat than "17 home toasters."³⁵

The Coca-Cola Company experienced one of the major marketing blunders of our generation when it tried to introduce "New" Coke. When it became clear that the strategy wasn't working, the company had to reintroduce the old stuff under a new name, Coca-Cola "Classic." The company said that " 'New' Coke, instead of being a 'flagship brand,' became a 'fighting brand' within a 'megabrand,' possessor of attributes that are a 'strategic plank' in Coke's total marketing scheme."³⁶ Nobody likes failure, and certainly nobody likes to admit they were part of one.

But failure is real, and very few things create more stress than failing while being taught by someone that God wants all His children to be successful. Our resident prophets of profit have conveniently ignored passages like Psalm 73:3-14:

For I was envious of the arrogant, as I saw the prosperity of the wicked. For there are no pains in their death; and their body is fat. They are not in trouble as other men; nor are they plagued like mankind. Therefore pride is their necklace; the garment of violence covers them. Their eye bulges from fatness; the imaginations of their heart run riot. They mock, and wickedly speak of oppression; they speak from on high. They have set their mouth against the heavens and their tongue parades through the earth. Therefore, his people return to this place; and waters of abundance are drunk by them. And they say, "How does God know? And is there knowledge with the Most High?" Behold, these are the wicked; and always at ease they have increased in wealth. Surely in vain I have kept my heart pure, and washed my hands in innocence; for I have been stricken all day long and chastened every morning.

All around us the wicked prosper. They are fat, they don't seem to be in trouble like the rest of us, and they mock God. They are at ease and keep increasing in wealth. However, believers suffer a different fate—we are stricken and chastened.

This is the reality of life. The righteous are not always rich. We have taken an idea that is part of our culture and turned it into a basis of faith. Consequently, we try to live by values that God never sanctioned. When we do, tremendous stress rises inside us as we worry about failure and try to succeed at all costs.

Called to be Different

We are quoted Bible verses as motivators to psych us into success. We are told that the promise to Joshua is ours to claim: "For then you will make your way prosperous, and then you will have success" (Joshua 1:8). Or Psalm 1:3 is a promise we can stand on: "And in whatever he does, he prospers." But Paul himself knew there was more to succeeding than simply having a positive attitude. In Romans 7:15 he writes, "For that which I am doing, I do not understand; for I am not practicing what I would like to do, but I am doing the very thing I hate." Attempts to succeed by self-effort are wrong—the unbeliever may briefly succeed with them, but they are ultimately doomed when used by a Christian. God wants us to rely on Him and His power. Our faith must be completely in Him, not a value system originated by the world, propagated by the world, and worshipped by the world. The Christian is called to be different — inherently and visibly.

We are to be different from those who value money as something with intrinsic worth, and from those who spend a lifetime amassing possessions so that they can affirm the validity of that somewhat serious bumper sticker: "He who dies with the most toys wins." We are to be different from those who value personal peace and security at any price. We must stand apart from those who would put work on a pedestal and make it everything — their god and idol. We should be committed enough to spend more time and effort seeking to advance the Kingdom of God than on anything else. And we must challenge the emphasis on success and the theology of wealth that has a virtual stranglehold on so many believers today.

Step #6 to Financial Freedom

Truthfully assess where your heart is, then challenge the value system of the world through the example of your life.

PART TWO

THE CALL
OF GOD

SEVEN

"LET EACH ONE OF YOU PUT ASIDE AND SAVE"

Giving

The Jerusalem Christians were in poverty. A number of different theories have been advanced to explain their condition. We too could speculate on why they had such great needs, but that is not a major issue for this study. Through their predicament, we can see how other Christians responded to their needs and used that response as a framework around which to build a biblical philosophy of giving.

The most extensive New Testament references to giving were written because of the situation in Jerusalem. In 2 Corinthians chapters 8 and 9 Paul urged the Corinthians to give toward the relief efforts in Jerusalem. However, Paul actually brought the subject up about one year earlier:

> Now concerning the collection for the saints, as I directed the churches of Galatia, so do you also. On the first day of every week let each one of you put aside and save, as he may prosper, that no collections be made when I come. And when I arrive, whomever you may approve, I shall send them with letters to carry your gift to Jerusalem (1 Corinthians 16:1-3).

There are three major points of note in these verses. The first is that Paul had directed the *churches* in Galatia to give. This is so often overlooked by the churches of our day. Our ethnocentricity frequently blinds us to the fact that we have a responsibility to reach beyond our own group, our church, our group of churches, or our denomination. Each church has a duty to look outside its walls when the needs of others are involved.

The second point concerns each individual's duty to give. Paul admonished everyone within the church to "put aside and save." There were no exceptions.

Jesus emphasized the same principle in Mark 12:41-44. In these verses we see Him sitting near the temple so that He can observe people putting money into the treasury. Mark tells us that many rich people were putting in very large amounts of money. No specific mention is made of any of the wealthy donors, however. The emphasis of the passage is on a poor widow who "came and put in two small copper coins, which amount to a cent."

These were probably the smallest copper coins in use at the time, similar to our own copper pennies. Why would Jesus think it so important to point out a woman putting two pennies into the temple treasury? Because she "put in all she owned, all she had to live on" (v. 44). Regardless of a person's financial position, he is still to give. Jesus praised the sacrifice of the widow in poverty, and Paul set forth the general principle instructing all Christians to give.

The third point to emerge from these verses is that giving should be on a regular basis. Paul asked the Corinthians to set something aside on the first day of every week. Although Paul prescribed a definite pattern for them to follow, we need not see this as a hard-and-fast rule that we should adhere to in a legalistic fashion. It so happened that the believers gathered for worship on the first day of the week (Acts 20:7) and it's safe to assume that those in Corinth were doing the same.

Regardless of when worship took place, the main point behind verse two seems to be "as he may prosper" rather than "on the first day of every week." If a person didn't make any money, he would obviously have nothing to give. However, if he had some financial success, he should give as soon after that as possible. The regular gatherings on the first of the week were logical places to give after a successful financial week.

Our giving should also be regular. As soon after we have received our paychecks or income from other sources, we should be in the habit of immediately writing out a check to those organizations that we support. The regularity of our gifts will depend on when we "prosper." For those who are salaried, it will probably mean giving twice a month. For others, it will depend on when income is received. Nevertheless, it should become habitual for us to give immediately when the Lord prospers us financially.

Apparently Paul had some other reasons for desiring regular giving. In 2 Corinthians 9:3,4, he told the Corinthians that he did not want to be put to shame by finding them unprepared with their gifts. Paul probably thought that a regular giving program by all the Christians would result in more gifts for the relief work in Jerusalem. If they were prepared to give when he came, he wouldn't be discredited.

Let me add one more bit of speculation as to why Paul wanted regular gifts. I would like to believe that he did not want to be forced to make a last-minute, emotional appeal for gifts. There is probably nothing inherently wrong with these types of appeals, but those who make them need to be cautious. Reliance must be placed on *God* to raise the needed funds and *not* on an individual's persuasive powers. The Lord should convict us to give after a thoughtful evaluation of the needs expressed and the alternatives for giving that are open to us. Giving on the basis of emotion only can frequently be an irresponsible use of our money. Being the one doing the persuading can be worse than irresponsible.

The Macedonian Approach

In spite of Paul's admonition in 1 Corinthians 16, the believers in Corinth did not give to the extent that Paul expected or thought they were capable of giving. In 2 Corinthians 8:10, 11, we read that they had been giving for about a year, but there was still need. They needed some additional prodding to motivate greater giving. Therefore, Paul wrote the eighth and ninth chapters of 2 Corinthians to lay down some more principles on giving and hopefully stimulate them to give greater amounts. He used the Macedonians as an example for the Corinthians to follow.

In the first five verses of chapter eight we see some interesting contrasts within the Macedonian church. They were afflicted yet joyful, and in a great deal of poverty yet liberal in their giving. Basically, they were in bad shape financially but had an unusual attitude toward giving — they were excited about it. They actually *begged* Paul to allow them to participate in the relief work for the Jerusalem Christians!

The Macedonians' attitude toward giving is directly opposed to the attitude we find among many of us today. How often do we beg to participate in a fundraising program? How often do we get genuinely excited about giving to the Lord's work? How often do we give beyond our ability? Usually our attitude is to take offense at requests for money. We become upset and angry because some "aggressive" pastor is "always asking for money."

We too can learn from the example of the Macedonians. Like those believers, we should be excited and enthusiastic about participating in a ministry through giving our funds. It might not be a bad idea to go so far as to thank those who receive our funds for having a ministry that is worth supporting.

The Macedonians were also great givers. Paul informs us that "their deep poverty overflowed in the wealth of their liberality." How were they able to give so much? What was their motivation?

In 2 Corinthians 8:1 we see that the grace of God played the primary role in motivating their gifts. It's not very surprising then to learn that His grace enables us to give back to Him what was really His in the first place. All of our wealth belongs to God. His grace gives it to us, and His grace empowers us to return it to Him.

The other great motivating factor behind the Macedonians' gifts is more within our control: "They first gave themselves to the Lord" (2 Corinthians 8:5). Their attitude about money and giving was formed only after they had placed themselves in the proper relationship with God. The actions of the Macedonians show us that a person's attitude toward giving reveals what is going on within his spiritual life. Thus, if we are not giving the way God intended us to, we have a spiritual problem and not a financial problem.

The fact that our handling of money is really an outward manifestation of the condition of our spirit is seen not only in regard to giving, but in more general areas of money management as well. Jesus points out in the parable of the talents (Matthew 25) that what we do with our money can be seen as a test of our faithfulness. Thanks to the example of the Macedonians, we now see that our responsibility is to get our relationship with God straight by giving *ourselves* to Him first. His grace will then enable us to give the money we should.

Who Do We Give To?

Part of what Paul has to say regarding gifts to the Jerusalem Christians involves an assurance to the Corinthians that their gifts will be administered properly. From these words we can see some general guidelines concerning administration that should be followed by Christian organizations and demanded by donors. The first guideline is found in verse nineteen of chapter eight where we read that the gift "is being administered by us for the glory of the Lord Himself."

The end result of our gifts should be the support of a ministry that is seeking to bring glory to God, not man. Thus, we should be very careful about our contributions to those who detract from the Lord by bringing an inordinate amount of attention to themselves. This is a very difficult area in which to give specific guidelines since each of us will have perceptions about when attention directed at individuals is really too much. Each of us will also have different opinions in certain areas regarding whether or not an action really brings glory to God. But perhaps Paul's other two points will give us more specific help.

The actual administration of the gift should be "honorable, not only in the sight of the Lord, but also in the sight of men" (2 Corinthians 8:21). The organization should adhere to honorable fundraising techniques and management practices. The funds should be disbursed properly into the areas directly related to the organization's ministry, and there should be a wise use of the funds at the administrative end of the organization. Obviously, we could elaborate, but suffice it to say that the donor should do a little homework on his own. Request information from the organization and talk to people who are involved. Don't give blindly to whatever happens to strike your fancy at the moment.

Finally, those who administer the gift should have been "often tested and found diligent in many things" (2 Corinthians 8:22). This is probably the most effective way to determine the quality of an organization. Do the leaders have spiritual maturity and integrity? Do they have a correct view of Scripture, and are they applying the principles within Scripture to their ministry? Do they have a good track record within their present ministry as well as during their prior activities? It may be difficult to answer all these questions satisfactorily, but again some effort and homework will certainly be helpful.

How Much Do We Give?

Whenever the subject of giving is discussed, the conversation eventually gets around to how much we should be giving. Paul did not give the Corinthians a fixed amount or percentage, but he did bring up three general principles that can be used as guidelines. The first is found in 2 Corinthians 8:13—the principle of equality.

The Corinthians had what Paul considered an "abundance" (v. 14). That abundance was present for the very purpose of providing for the needs of those who were lacking. There should be a sharing between those who have and those who do not have so that an equitable balance can be achieved. Paul's authority for this principle is in Exodus 16 where the Israelites gathered just enough manna to supply their daily needs, no one falling short and no one having a surplus. Thus, the Lord wanted everyone to be taken care of.

The Jerusalem Christians were not being provided for, and it was the responsibility of fellow believers who had adequate provisions to supply their needs. There should be a more equal distribution of assets. However, this principle of equality does present to us at least two problems. The first is that it is conceivable that we could give away all that we own and never fully equalize our wealth with that of our poorer brothers and sisters. Should we therefore give away all that we own?

In Luke 18 Jesus asks the "rich young ruler" to sell all that he has and give it to the poor. Only then will he be able to enter the Kingdom of God. The ruler wouldn't do it.

We have already seen in Mark 12 Jesus' praise for the widow who did give away all that she owned. This story and the preceding one would seem to argue for such actions. But another event is often overlooked whenever we are challenged with these passages. This story is told only verses after the one about the rich young ruler.

In the first ten verses of Luke 19 we read about the conversion of Zaccheus. "He was a chief tax-gatherer, and he was rich" (v. 2). However, Luke records that Zaccheus gave only half his possessions to the poor, yet Jesus said, "Today salvation has come to this house" (v. 9).

Giving half of all that we own would still be a significant step. But the fact that these two stories are so close together in the Scriptures and each elicited a different response from Jesus — one man was asked to give up all, he wouldn't and was rejected; another gave up half voluntarily and was accepted — indicates that the amount we give in response to the principle of equality must be an individual decision. This may mean that some of us are indeed commanded to give up all that we have. We need to be careful because Scripture isn't clear. For some Christians, this type of radical discipleship may not be an option but an obedient response to the Lord's command. It is for this reason that the story of the rich young ruler should not be overly spiritualized or rationalized. Giving away all possessions should be considered a possible option for some.

For others the story of Zaccheus may be more appropriate. They may be commanded to give away significant amounts but not everything. They will have to balance the amount of their gifts with Paul's words that giving "is not for the ease of others and for your affliction" (2 Corinthians 8:13). If you will have to incur debt in order to give, or if you are giving so much that you and your family are afflicted to the point of needing relief funds, then you have gone too far. After all, Paul did not ask the Corinthians to give away everything that they had. He could have, but he also wrote that our wealth must be available to provide for the needs of our own families (1 Timothy 5:8) and he undoubtedly knew Ecclesiastes 5:19, which indicates that our wealth is to supply our own needs as well.

Nevertheless, there is a tension in the principle of equality that all of us must realize and give serious thought to. Some believers are called to give away all possessions. Others must balance the needs that they feel God has compelled them to provide for within their families with the needs of those in this world who do not have as much wealth. Each one of us should think through carefully what God would have us do in this area.

The second problem with equality can be phrased as: How do we in our capitalistic society respond to the communal lifestyle found in Acts 2:43-45? The believers in the early church sold all their property and possessions and shared them with everyone. To some extent we have already spoken to that question when we looked at the pros and cons of giving away everything. Our answer here must be similar too. Some of us will be called to sell everything, some will not. But surely all of us must be open to sharing our possessions with other believers. It may be something as simple as a flashlight or as valuable as an automobile. We should even be willing to open our homes to relieve certain needs. Sharing with other Christians should become a part of our fellowship, something we are willing and eager to do for those who have certain needs or just do not have an item they could use at the time. It may even include sharing our meals with others.

If a communal lifestyle or an organized program of sharing possessions is to be implemented, it is important to remember that it should not be forced on people. This brings us to the second general principle that Paul uses as a guideline on how much to give. Each one of us should "do just as he has purposed in his heart; not grudgingly or under compulsion; for God loves a cheerful giver" (2 Corinthians 9:7). We should give what God convicts us to give, such things as force or a desire to keep up with our friends should not be factors.

The third principle is to give bountifully. "Now this I say, he who sows sparingly shall also reap sparingly; and he who sows bountifully shall also reap bountifully" (2 Corinthians 9:6). We shouldn't hold back on our gifts; we should make very generous and liberal ones. Now we have three of Paul's principles regarding how much we should give—the principles of equality, giving what God convicts us to give, and bountiful giving. These three principles should be ingrained in our attitude toward stewardship. But unfortunately this hasn't happened throughout the body of Christ. All of us can probably think of objections we have heard to each principle: "I'm so poor that equality means somebody should give to me"; "God hasn't convicted me to give anything yet"; "I don't have enough to give bountifully." They are all nice objections but will not stand up under the test of Scripture. Each one of us is called to start giving at some level. That level is the tithe.

What About the Tithe?

The first time the tithe appears in Scripture is in Genesis 14:17-20. Abram had just returned from defeating those who had taken Lot. Melchizedek met him, and Hebrews 7:4 tells us that Abram gave him a "tenth of the choicest spoils."

Over the years the tithe developed into a very legalistic system. Jesus shows us what had happened by His day in Matthew 23:23: "Woe to you, scribes and Pharisees, hypocrites! For you tithe mint and dill and cummin, and have neglected the weightier provisions of the law: justice and mercy and faithfulness; but these are the things you should have done without neglecting the others." Mint, dill, and cummin were three herbs of the kitchen garden. A tithe on them would be extremely small, much like our tithing the alfalfa sprouts that are frequently grown in kitchen windows today. Legally, the scribes and Pharisees were right in making their small tithes. But they were paying too much attention to something that wasn't really meaningful while ignoring those parts of the law that were. The sad thing is that this kind of legalistic adherence to the tithe while conveniently ignoring more important laws had been going on at least as far back as the time when Amos wrote. In the fourth chapter of Amos we read that the tithe was kept regularly, but the people were living extravagant lifestyles and oppressing the poor. Apparently things had not changed much when Jesus appeared.

Matthew 23:23 is the only direct mention of the tithe that Jesus makes. However, this does not clearly tell us whether or not the tithe still applies to the Christian today. Does it? The answer is very definite: yes and no.

Jesus' statement in the Sermon on the Mount that He came to fulfill the Law is well-known: "Do not think that I came to abolish the Law or the Prophets; I did not come to abolish, but to fulfill" (Matthew 5:17). For the rest of chapter five He gives us examples of the ways that the Old Testament Law is fulfilled. There are six specific examples, and in every case the Law of the Old Testament is expanded. "You shall not commit murder" becomes, "everyone who is angry with his brother shall be guilty." "You shall not commit adultery" becomes, "everyone who looks on a woman to lust for her has committed adultery with her already in his heart." "An eye for an eye, and a tooth for a tooth" is now, "do not resist him who is evil; but whoever slaps you on your right cheek, turn to him the other also."

True, the tithe is not mentioned in any of the six examples. However, at no point in the New Testament is it overruled, either directly or indirectly, as some of the Old Testament laws are. I believe we can view the tithe in the same light as the six examples. It is a minimum, a starting point. We are to go beyond the tithe if we intend to fulfill its purpose.

Now we have the answer to our question: Does the tithe apply today? Yes it does, but no it doesn't, because we are to go much further in our giving. Many of us see the tithe as a goal to reach, a place in our giving where we would eventually like to be. That's the wrong view to take. The tithe must be seen as a place to *begin*. Our goal must be set at some point in excess of the tithe. How much in excess? Here is where the three principles we discussed earlier come into play. The principles of giving to achieve equality, giving what God convicts us to give, and giving bountifully must now be considered as we decide how much in excess of the tithe we are to give.

Even though the tithe should only be considered a minimum, a certain "Christian legalism" can be found today wherever people are still attached to the tithe. The problem can be phrased as this question: Should I tithe on my net income or gross income?

The answer depends on who you are. If you are an independent businessman, there is a possibility that you will not be able to give 10 percent of your gross earnings. The expenses incurred in running the business may be so large that net earnings are small, if present at all. It may therefore be impossible to give 10 percent of gross.

On the other hand those on a salary should be tithing on their gross pay. In Proverbs 3:9 we are directed to honor the Lord from the "first of all [our] produce." It is merely because our government has legislated itself into first place that we receive a paycheck with the taxes removed. The actions of a human government are not legitimate reasons for placing the Lord second. We should not be blinded by the government's legislative claim to the first of our produce. The Lord still reigns supreme, and it is to Him that we owe our primary allegiance in all things.

Giving More than the Tithe

The Old Testament also notes that there was more to giving than the tithe. Offerings and sacrifices were integral parts of Jewish worship. There were burnt offerings, peace offerings, offerings of the first born, votive and freewill offerings, offerings of first fruits, guilt, sin, grain, and meal offerings. The Jews were expected to perform all of these offerings that were over and above the tithe.

Obviously, some of these offerings and sacrifices are no longer needed because of Jesus' work on the cross. This can be seen clearly in Hebrews where we read that the blood of Jesus and not the blood of animals cleanses us now (Hebrews 9:13, 14). Also, the "Law, since it has only a shadow of the good things to come and not the very form of things, can never by the same sacrifices year by year, which they offer continually, make perfect those who draw near" (Hebrews 10:1).

The specific offerings and sacrifices of the Old Testament may not be needed, but the concept of offerings and sacrifices still remains, only in different forms. As the New Testament expands the Old Testament law on tithing, so it also expands the old ideas of offerings and sacrifices through new forms. It may be as obvious as sacrificial gifts in excess of the tithe, or it may be in ways that require us to do certain things that will not be easy. These are areas of sacrifice and giving back to the Lord, aspects of giving that go beyond money.

Sacrificial Giving

Unfortunately, many discussions on giving are confined to the financial aspects. The biblical philosophy of giving goes beyond money. There are at least four areas of giving that the Bible calls "sacrifices." The first relates to making our bodies sacrifices and is found in Romans 12:1: "I urge you therefore, brethren, by the mercies of God, to present your bodies a living and holy sacrifice, acceptable to God, which is your spiritual service of worship."

The second sacrifice is to "continually offer up a sacrifice of praise to God" (Hebrews 13:15).

Third, "do not neglect doing good and sharing; for with such sacrifices God is pleased" (Hebrews 13:16). Here we can clearly see that giving is more than money — it's time too. Actions of service on our part are frequently sacrifices because they take time, something most of us have less of than money. Yet God calls us to sacrifice our time for others. This is an area of giving that should not be neglected.

The fourth sacrifice is the ultimate sacrifice. Paul, a prisoner who realizes his death is close, writes to Timothy: "For I am already being poured out as a drink offering, and the time of my departure has come" (2 Timothy 4:6). Reading this should cause us to realize that we too may be called to offer our lives as sacrifices.

These four New Testament sacrifices are presented to stress that giving goes beyond money. It involves our bodies, our praise, our time in acts of service, and perhaps our very lives. Money is only the beginning for each of us.

Why Give?

So far we've looked at some general principles on giving, what it takes to give sacrificially, who we should give to, and how much we should give. Let's return now to 2 Corinthians 9 and see what Paul says about why we should give. He cites at least three reasons.

The first and most obvious is to supply the material needs of others (2 Corinthians 9:12). The second is so that the giver may receive and be enriched (vv. 6, 10, 11). However, we must be very careful when applying these verses and using this reason as one for our giving. Of all the teaching that has been done on giving, this is the point that has been stretched out of proportion to its importance. It has been misused, and misapplied. It has reached the point of becoming a rival theology nurtured by the materialistic ethic of our culture and directly at odds with much of Scripture. Many of us who have bought into this theology are doing nothing more than living lives centered on ourselves.

One popular Christian organization now teaches,

> When you give a tithe or offering you should expect to get . . . .
> You can expect people to give things to you . . . . There is a
> ratio of blessings . . . . Give five dollars, get five dollars.

The conclusion: it is Scriptural to give in order to receive.

An author who was disturbed by this type of philosophy
offered these words as his concept of the testimony being created
today: "After I was saved and began giving to Christian work,
God blessed me in a new way and prospered me so that now I'm
enjoying the good things of life (better car, larger house, costlier
vacations) more than ever before."[1]

One of the fallacies of this theory is that it assumes God will
only bless us with material goods. Again, our society's concepts
of success and blessings have influenced us. God's blessings are
not necessarily material goods. But the greatest fallacy of this
theory lies in the inability of those who espouse it to see God's
purpose in bestowing on them a material blessing.

God does want to bless us for our gifts, and in many cases
(but not all) we will receive material blessings. However, His
purpose in returning material goods to us is so that we will continue to benefit and bless others. Just as we are responsible for
making gifts to God, so we are also responsible for the wise use
of gifts we receive from God, even those resulting from our gifts.
This will not mean bigger, better, or faster material goods. It will
mean an expanded giving program that considers the Lord's
desires and the well-being of others before ourselves.

The final reason for giving is a spiritual one. This is the
greatest reason and the one that each of us should strive to concentrate on whenever we make gifts to the Lord's work. Paul
shows us how wonderful this reason is in 2 Corinthians 9:12-14:

> For the ministry of this service is not only fully supplying the
> needs of the saints, but is also overflowing through many
> thanksgivings to God. Because of the proof given by this min-
> istry they will glorify God for your obedience to your confes-
> sion of the gospel of Christ, and for the liberality of your con-
> tribution to them and to all, while they also, by prayer on
> your behalf, yearn for you because of the surpassing grace of
> God in you.

In these verses we find a reason for giving that is far greater than the two others we have discussed. Unfortunately, this is the reason that is most often ignored. Too many of us see giving as a burden that cramps our lifestyle or as an obligation—something we have to do because we are Christians. This is not giving the way God intended. Our act of giving is a privilege of our commitment as believers. It is done to enrich the soul of the giver, relieve the needs of others, and bring an "overflow" of praise and gratitude to God. "Thanks be to God for His indescribable gift!" (v. 15).

Postscript

What finally happened to the Corinthians? Did they give? We find that answer in Romans 15:26: "For Macedonia and Achaia have been pleased to make a contribution for the poor among the saints in Jerusalem." (The province of Achaia was governed from Corinth, and that word generally refers to Corinth.)

Apparently Paul's exhortation was effective. The Corinthians are spoken of together with the Macedonians as being "pleased" to give to the relief work in Jerusalem. We can only guess what their attitude was as they made the gifts but would hope that it came close to being like that of the Macedonians.

We can learn much from the Macedonians too. Let's take their excitement about giving to the Lord and bring it into the twentieth century. Let's give ourselves to Him so that His grace will allow us to give what we should—never forgetting that we are only returning to God what He has given us. After all, God owns everything. We owe Him no less than everything.

Step #7 to Financial Freedom

Get in the habit of giving more than 10 percent regardless of your circumstances.

EIGHT

"DO NOT BE ANXIOUS FOR TOMORROW"

Faith

In 1984 three young men left what they were doing to follow what they believed to be God's leading into a new business arena. One had been in the newspaper business, another in construction, and a third at a law firm. I was the third one. Each of us was certain that God wanted us in real estate development.

We started with ideas and desires, but no land or projects. Many times each day we came to the Lord seeking His direction toward our first project. After months of our prayers and searching for just the right location, He led us to a small retail site.

The next obstacle was money. We had no equity to put into the project, and we needed a solid banking relationship. So it was decided to raise equity from investors. We put together a limited partnership and began to seek out people who would invest with us. But as the time approached when we had to close on the land, it was clear that we didn't have enough. Unless we raised another $48,000, we would lose our chance to get the land.

We continued to pray and seek the Lord. Time was quickly running out. Soon it was the day before we needed the money and unless God provided, all would be lost. Miraculously, He did — and with only thirty minutes left to spare! There was no question in any of our minds that God had provided that $48,000.

Over the next few months we witnessed many similar miracles. We needed a total of $600,000 in equity for the project. Every day, either individually or together, we sought the Lord many times. Slowly and steadily the money came in. Much of it was from our friends and fellow church members. Many of them prayed about their involvement in the project and felt led to invest.

We also saw some remarkable events occur during the construction. Time and time again God's hand was made evident.

As the project took shape the company also grew. We added employees and moved to larger quarters at a more central location. The Lord brought to us another slightly larger retail project that we took on with enthusiasm.

Next we branched out into industrial project development. Our third project was less costly than the second so we felt comfortable with it. We also knew that the financial markets were beginning to tighten up and that finding financing would be difficult. But God had provided for us before, and we knew He would again.

Remarkably, we were able to secure a type of prelease agreement on almost 70 percent of the space. In the market we were operating that was considered phenomenal.

Once again we went to a limited partnership for equity and again God blessed us. Some of our earlier investors decided to put funds into this project, and we continued to see a prayerful consideration by many regarding their involvement with us.

During this time we made one more real estate investment. It was a small tract of land that we bought personally. We intended to hold this for a few years and then sell it or seek other partners to help us with the payments. But things were beginning to fall apart. Real estate development was dying due to overbuilding and a change in the tax laws. We couldn't find good opportunities, investors, or lenders. Our company income fell to nothing, and the projects were facing serious problems.

Without income it was apparent that overhead had to be cut. One by one we began laying off employees. It was a gutwrenching experience. These people had become our friends. They too had felt God leading them to us and were absolutely convinced it was His will for them to be a part of the company and grow with it.

The company grew all right—in reverse. After we lost our people, there still wasn't enough money to meet other obligations. We had a lease car that was taken back. The rent on our own space was much too high so we had to default on the lease and move out. We believed that God would at least provide enough money for us to meet our commitments, but it just didn't come. No amount or intensity of prayer or work produced enough funds for those obligations.

The projects were also in trouble. We couldn't make the payments on our land, find partners, sell it, or renegotiate the loan. Consequently, it was foreclosed on, and we lost tens of thousands of dollars. Our second project was suffering serious negative cash flow problems, but fortunately we were able to sell it to another investment group. God delivered us from that liability. Our third project lost all but one of its pre-leased tenants. When construction was finished, the occupancy rate was 7 percent. We sold our joint venture interest to keep the project alive, and so far our investors have retained their interest. But the ultimate outcome is yet to be decided, and it appears that, at best, it will be many, many years before a return to the investors is ever realized.

Leasing on our first project remained at just below break-even for many months. Our lender had been approaching insolvency and that restricted its ability to work with us. Our lender put intense pressure on us to make timely payments. The original lender was eventually merged into another bank. The center lost its anchor tenant and that made it impossible for us to work out an agreement with the bank. They took it back through foreclosure. We and the investors lost everything — hundreds of thousands of dollars.

Why has God allowed this? Specifically, why did God provide projects, money, funding, and employees only to have us lose them, default on some obligations, and fail at most of what we set out to do?

On a more general level, why does God allow financial losses and failures? Why does He allow financial pressures to be constantly eating away at us?

To this point we have looked at many of the causes of financial pressures. Now we will address the more difficult and seemingly illogical question of why financial pressures come even when we have our financial priorities in order. Why are we still under pressure when we have done everything that a righteous person can do?

Failure

God wills failure. That's a tough statement, but I'm convinced that it's true. For the last few years I operated under the assumption that if God caused one good thing to happen, He would certainly follow that with another good thing — or at least allow a good thing to happen in the end. We miraculously obtained our 10 percent down payment on the first project thirty minutes before the deadline. Through the years we raised over $1 million from investors, many of whom were fellow believers who prayed earnestly about their participation in our projects and concluded that was where God wanted their money. We got financing on our third project during a market when loans just weren't being made for that sort of thing. And we earnestly prayed daily, as a team and as individuals, for the projects to work. All these things led us to believe that God was with us and would surely give us a successful conclusion to the projects.

Yet He led us into unfulfilled hopes, losses, and failures. Oh, I suppose we could have always tried a little harder or worked a little longer. But we surely did virtually everything we could do to make the projects and the company work. The only conclusion is that failure can be just as much ordained by God as is success.

That leads us to the next question: What is failure? In the world's eyes it may be bankruptcy, foreclosure, losing a case, losing a job, etc. — all are usually considered failures. But if God ordains them, perhaps our labeling of those events as "failures" is wrong.

The True Standard of Success

One of the problems lies in what we have been led to believe is the true standard of success. Vernon Grounds described it when he wrote about the man the world judges as a success in private life: "He earns enough money to meet his needs and even gratify some of his desires. His neighbors respect him, his friends like him, his family loves him. He enjoys a maximum of pleasures and suffers a minimum of pains. He has good health and peace of mind. He is free from guilt, depression, or regrets. At a ripe old age he dies in his sleep, is decently buried, and is mourned." Then Grounds looked at the one considered successful in public life: "To be publicly successful someone must be superior in some way — in beauty, brains, or brawn. Such a person has a higher status in society. He is admired, perhaps envied. Popularity, fame, influence, political power, rare creativity, enormous wealth — these mark the successful person."[1]

However, since God does put the Christian into a position where he is not viewed as a worldly success, where he doesn't earn enough money, or where he loses investments, cars, and homes and falls into bankruptcy, then it is not the success or the failure that matters. Each has a higher purpose.

In order to see that purpose, we must first realize that God's standards are different from the world's. Paul writes about this in 1 Corinthians:

> Where is the wise man? Where is the scribe? Where is the debater of this age? Has not God made foolish the wisdom of the world? For since in the wisdom of God the world through its wisdom did not come to know God, God was well-pleased through the foolishness of the message preached to save those who believe . . . but God has chosen the foolish things of the world to shame the wise, and God has chosen the weak things of the world to shame the things which are strong, and the base things of the world and the despised, God has chosen, the things that are not, that He might nullify the things that are, that no man should boast before God . . . For the wisdom of this world is foolishness before God. For it is written, "He is the one who catches the wise in their craftiness" (1 Corinthians 1:20, 21, 27-29; 3:19).

God has turned everything around. What is success in the world's eyes may very well be failure, and what is failure to the world may be success to God. Consider the hall of faith in Hebrews 11. We tend to overlook verses thirty-two through thirty-eight. Surely these people would have been considered failures by their world: "And others experienced mockings and scourgings, yes, also chains and imprisonment. They were stoned, they were sawn in two, . . . they were put to death with the sword; they went about in sheepskins, in goatskins, being destitute, afflicted, ill-treated (men of whom the world was not worthy), wandering in deserts and mountains and caves and holes in the ground" (Hebrews 11:36-38).

They were "men of whom the world was not worthy." Isn't that a remarkable statement? They weren't worthy of the world, yet what do you think the world thought of them? They were outcasts and derelicts, not even worth thinking about.

These people had an extraordinary faith. They knew God's standard of success, and they held onto it tenaciously. They had the faith to face failure.

Useful to God

I'm not sure that we have that kind of faith today. The world seems almost too powerful, even in our churches. We readily acknowledge that the cross is foolishness to men and wisdom to God while failing to realize that other things that are foolish and useless to men are wise and useful to God. He can use failure just as readily as He can success.

Perhaps God could use failure even more than success. After all, more people have experienced failure and mediocrity than success. We might consider the words of Paul: "I have become all things to all men that I may by all means save some" (1 Corinthians 9:22). In order to reach people, we must become like them. That's clear in cross-cultural ministries. It's less clear when we think about our witness at home.

We look at failure as a chance to grow or bounce back with new lessons learned. It is that. But look at the focus — it continues to be on ourselves. We are encouraged by businessmen who have tried and failed many times only to learn and be ultimately successful. Those are nice stories but few people are able to do that. Most fail or continue to live in mediocrity. We view those conditions as something that God doesn't want. We've forgotten our primary responsibility of reaching the lost. For if most of the world lives in mediocrity, how are we to reach them?

Here is one of the problems: we look only at ourselves and how we are affected by failures. We must turn that around and look at how we can influence others by our failures. We are primarily witnesses — not businessmen, lawyers, doctors, clerks, etc. Our failures are tools for the task of witnessing. They may or may not help in our professions in the future. That doesn't matter as much as how we use them to advance the Kingdom.

Another problem is our misuse of Scripture. One example that I frequently hear is, "Beloved, I pray that in all respects you may prosper and be in good health, just as your soul prospers" (3 John 1:2). That's a nice prayer, but it's certainly no promise that all Christians will prosper financially. It's more like our comment, "I wish you every success." You can't build a prosperity theology on it.

A third problem is our belief in the power of positive thinking. Since our society has no faith in God as its base, all faith must be channeled into virtual worship of our achievements. This is expressed through the many promotions of self-confidence, belief in yourself, positive thinking, and possibility thinking as the ways to achieve financial success. The pressure from the world to succeed using these methods is intense. It's so great that it's easy to forget God and try to make it on our own.

Positive thinking isn't new. Job tried it and found that it didn't work: "Though I say, 'I will forget my complaint, I will leave off my sad countenance and be cheerful,' I am afraid of all my pains, I know that Thou wilt not acquit me" (Job 9:27, 28). Don't get too discouraged when you find that positive thinking doesn't work.

Finally, we must realize that we are not exempt from economic events in our world. Even as the rain falls on the just and the unjust (Matthew 5:45), so can foreclosure. When the stock market collapses, everybody loses money — not just unbelievers. Jesus Himself acknowledged this reality when He asked, "Do you suppose that those eighteen on whom the tower in Siloam fell and killed them, were worse culprits than all the men who live in Jerusalem?" (Luke 13:4).

Eliphaz the Temanite, in counseling Job, wondered, "Who ever perished being innocent, or where were the upright destroyed? According to what I have seen, those who plow iniquity and those who sow trouble harvest it" (Job 4:7,8). Eliphaz's powers of observation weren't too good. Unfortunately, the innocent do perish and the upright are destroyed. Failure does not belong only to those who plow iniquity. Sometimes they even succeed.

However, God doesn't see failure and losing money the same way we do. Consider the bad investment made by King Amaziah. Amaziah hired 100,000 warriors from Israel and paid them 100

talents of silver—over $500,000 in today's money. But a man of
God came to him and told him not to let the men of Israel go
with him since God was not with Israel. Amaziah replied by asking what he would do for all the money he had just given the
troops. The man of God answered, "The Lord has much more to
give you than this" (2 Chronicles 25:5-10).

A bad investment isn't the end of the world. Failure isn't
beyond the power of God to control. He may indeed lead us into
what the world considers failure. But it doesn't mean that we are
out of His will or that He cares less for us. He has more to give
us than money or a profitable investment.

A few years ago Sheldon Vanauken wrote a poignant and insightful book about the death of his wife. He related his experiences and feelings as her illness progressed and eventually led to
her death. Throughout this time he corresponded with C. S.
Lewis, who had been through a similar experience with his wife.
In one of the letters Lewis termed their trials "a severe mercy."

Failure is often like that. The events and situations through
which we must go are intense and severe. They can tear our
emotions, isolate us from friends, and devastate our lives. We
can reach depths of despair that we never dreamed of before. Yet
in the midst of severity, God remains merciful. Failure is also "a
severe mercy."

Anticipating God

God wants us to have the faith to face failure. Success isn't
always decreed for the Christian. But there are other aspects of
our faith that God wants to test. He wants to see just how long
we are willing to wait and depend on Him.

Saul knew what it was like to give up and stop waiting. The
Philistines had assembled 30,000 chariots, 6,000 horsemen, and
"people like the sand which is on the seashore in abundance." The
people of Israel saw their plight and hid themselves or ran away.

Samuel had told Saul to wait at Gilgal for seven days. Saul
waited and waited and waited, but Samuel didn't come. The
people were starting to scatter. Saul had to do something soon or
he would lose everybody. So he decided to offer the burnt offering and peace offering, even though that was not the right thing
to do. As soon as Saul offered the burnt offering, Samuel walked

up. Saul offered his explanation—"you [Samuel] did not come within the appointed days"—but it was not acceptable. Samuel replied that if Saul could have waited, God would have established his kingdom over Israel forever. Instead, God chose another man to bless and through whom would come the Savior (1 Samuel 13:5-14).

Saul anticipated God and lost the chance to have his kingdom established forever. Even though Samuel didn't come when he said he would, Saul still should have waited for God's provision. It was not Saul's place to make the offerings. He just couldn't wait long enough.

The Right Timing

When we anticipate God, the consequences may not be so drastic. However, we still may be forfeiting God's blessing. The loss of a job may be so hard on us or the fear of no income may grip us so tightly that we feel compelled to find another job immediately. In our own power we may be able to do that. But it might not be what God wants for us. He could have something better if we wait for His direction, seek His counsel, and sense His peace when the timing is right. Then there are times when the pressures mount and we work harder and harder only to find ourselves falling further and further behind. Or we think that our present job can never provide enough income to meet our needs so we quit and go looking for another one.

In times like these God wants us to slow down and seek Him. Although He may want us to seek another, higher paying job, He may also want us to cut back our "needs" or wait for Him to provide more income at our present job. Unless we wait for His answer we will not know. As George Mueller has said,

> the natural mind is ever prone to reason, when we ought to believe; to be at work when we ought to be quiet; to go our own way, when we ought steadily to walk on in God's ways, however trying to nature. . . . When we . . . anticipate God, by going our own way . . . we certainly weaken faith instead of increasing it; and each time we work thus a deliverance of our own we find it more and more difficult to trust in God.[2]

Sometimes even the most logical choice is not the right one. There is a school of thought on discerning God's will that says use only our logic and intellect — a reasoned analysis of the problem must be correct. But this fails to take into account Proverbs 3:5: "Trust in the Lord with all your heart, and do not lean on your own understanding."

I am not saying that we shouldn't use our logic and intellect. But we must realize that they are human and therefore flawed. If we are depending *only* on our own understanding, what appears to be the most logical solution may not always be right. The only way to know is to seek the Lord and wait on His direction. Don't act on a decision simply because it seems to be the most logical without waiting for God's confirmation first. Let Jeremiah's words sink in: "I know, O Lord, that a man's way is not in himself; nor is it in a man who walks to direct his steps" (Jeremiah 10:23).

Problems with Presumption

It's one thing to wait and have faith in God; it's another to think we have faith when we act. The latter can be very dangerous and in reality can be nothing more than presumption. Frequently there is a fine line between faith and presumption. But through experience, counsel of mature, nonimpulsive Christians, and sensitivity to the Spirit, and an intense study of what Scripture really says, we must learn where that line is drawn. Proverbs 13:10 warns us about it: "Through presumption comes nothing but strife, but with those who receive counsel is wisdom." James gives us an example:

> Come now, you who say, "Today or tomorrow, we shall go to such and such a city, and spend a year there and engage in business and make a profit." Yet you do not know what your life will be like tomorrow. You are just a vapor that appears for a little while and then vanishes away (James 4:13, 14).

Another good example of presumption is "doing something on the come" — investing time or money in a project on nothing more than a hope that the resources will appear to pay for your efforts. Often I have seen people invest or spend money on personnel, equipment, or jobs because they believed God would honor them and wouldn't let them fail, or He would eventually use those things for their success. But God doesn't work that way. He honors faith in *Him*, not faith in what we want Him to be or do. Presumption assumes that the things we want are things He wants for us too. I suppose in a way that's faith—faith in an object—but not faith in God. There is a lot of that kind of confusion today. Much of what we call faith is often presumption.

So how do we distinguish between faith and presumption? I've come up with a six-point scenario that's been very helpful to follow when it is time to make a decision:

1. *Pray* for the wisdom to sort through and analyze facts, motives, desires, emotions, etc.—everything that creates a decision.

2. *Patience.* Too many times we are prompted to act by something that says, "Hurry, hurry!" More often than not, waiting clears up most questions and takes the urgency away from the situation. How long is long enough? Until you have a peace within you that God is leading you to proceed. There are no nice, neat, absolute formulas.

3. *Think.* During this waiting time, again analyze all the facts, motives, and so on.

4. When all the facts are in, *pray again.* Ultimately the decision must be from God, regardless of the facts.

5. *More patience.* Again this is needed. Don't move until you feel at peace emotionally and intellectually.

6. *Act.*

Patience, Patience, Patience

As you can see, I've put a lot of emphasis on patience. So does Scripture.

The plans of the diligent lead surely to advantage, but everyone who is hasty comes surely to poverty (Proverbs 21:5).

A tranquil heart is life to the body, but passion is rottenness to the bones (Proverbs 14:30).

For thus the Lord God, the Holy One of Israel, has said, "In repentance and rest you shall be saved, in quietness and trust is
your strength" (Isaiah 30:15).

In our society where everybody is striving to be the best,
reach the top, and work harder than the next guy, it's tough to be
quiet and patient. There's no room any more for reflection and
waiting. The salesman is told that making a sale is all in the
numbers so never let a minute go by without making another
phone call. There's not enough money for a new stereo system so
I'll work a little longer this month or get another job. The car has
to be washed and the yard mowed; I can't stop to meditate.

I noticed something very interesting as our real estate business
was collapsing and we were wondering where our next paychecks
were going to come from. All the positive things happening and
new business coming my way were things I had done virtually
nothing to get. They literally fell into my hands. Yet the work I
strove for produced nothing. The things for which we ran ads in
the paper and sent out a hundred mailers a week were unpro-
ductive. Striving and effort had little effect, but prayer and patience brought provision for my needs.

I wasn't completely inactive in the areas that were productive. Ecclesiastes 11:1 says, "Cast your bread on the surface of
the waters, for you will find it after many days." I was casting in
a lot of places. But the least results were obtained where I spent
the most human effort. That's been a great lesson to me regarding prayer and patience. God wants us to come to Him, wait on
Him, and let Him provide for us in His own way and in His
own time.

Uncertainty

When I first began to think about what to say on faith, I felt
very uncomfortable since so many of my financial problems
were not resolved. I suppose I was waiting for God to resolve
them all so I could write a glowing book about how God works
to solve all our problems. I could give a day-by-day analysis of
one of the real estate projects and then come to the end and say
God brought a buyer, made a big profit for our investors, and
saved us. That would have been wonderful.

However, would I still love God as much if He didn't deliver me into a successful conclusion? Would I still love Him even if I didn't see a fantastic miracle of deliverance?

Faith, very frequently, has nothing to do with deliverance (as we see it) or resolution. Consider Abraham, Isaac, and Jacob: "All these died in faith, without receiving the promises, but having seen them and welcomed them from a distance, and having confessed that they were strangers and exiles on the earth" (Hebrews 11:13). Consider Moses who never set foot in the promised land.

There are, of course, many who did receive promises and see great workings of God. By faith they escaped the sword, the weak were made strong, and women received back their dead. Yet we do overlook those in the last part of Hebrews 11 who were considered worldly failures and whose only deliverance from slow, painful torture was death. The prospect of martyrdom is a distant thought in our culture.

But reflection on the possible ultimate cost of our commitment to Christ should help us realize that regardless of our financial situation, money is not to be a priority in our lives. We've put Mammon before God too many times. There is no place for reversed priorities in the Kingdom.

Further, the end result of our struggles, financial or otherwise, may not be what we expect it to be. There may not even be an end as we perceive it. Faith does not depend on reaching an end, fulfilling of a promise, or realizing our desires. Faith is dealing with uncertainty. This is a key point. Too often we see faith as just hanging in there long enough to make it. The financial condition will get better, the job will improve, or God will deliver us out of our unpleasant situation. That's not always the case. The financial situation may not get better. We may be pondering where tomorrow's meal is coming from the rest of our lives. Faith is the "assurance of things hoped for, the conviction of things not seen" (Hebrews 11:1).

Our lives may be a day-to-day, hand-to-mouth existence until we die. We may never like everything about our jobs. It may be years before all our debts can be paid off. Those are the kinds of realizations that are so difficult to accept. Our fear of uncertainty and worry over the possibility that our financial problems may never be fully resolved can create tremendous emotional pressures if we try to bear the burden on our own.

That is why Jesus wants us to live one day at a time, and talk about our concerns with unconditionally supportive Christian friends. That really is an essential part of the cure for anxiety. The other part of the cure for anxiety is to try to do what we can. We shouldn't worry that we won't be able to pay off all our debts next year. We shouldn't worry about potential loss of income or inability to pay bills next month. We should only thank God that we made it through today. We made it — *today*! We ate — *today*! We paid our bills — *today*! God provided — *today*!

Helping Our Unbelief

Most of us acknowledge the truth in this. But how in the world do we get that from our heads to our hearts? We're like the man who said to Jesus, "I do believe; help my unbelief" (Mark 9:24).

The Israelites learned through experience. For forty years they were only given enough food for each day. The Lord told Moses, "Behold, I will rain bread from heaven for you; and the people shall go out and gather a day's portion every day, that I may test them, whether or not they will walk in My instruction" (Exodus 16:4).

We are only capable of learning to trust when we *have* to trust. God allows us, like the Israelites, to go through times of crises and pressures when we must trust Him or fall away. He wants to test us, to see whether or not we will obey Him.

This is "life on the edge." It's usually characterized by constant uncertainty and fear that we won't make it. It could mean a continuing battle to make ends meet, find more work, raise more money, or make more sales — all under the ever-present threat of falling over the edge of the precipice into financial ruin if everything doesn't go just right.

After living on the edge for a while, you begin to see that there is absolutely no other reason for being there than the fact that it's God's will. Our Lord is a gracious and compassionate God. Your remaining in an unresolved state for so long must mean that He has a purpose in it. Our Lord is also a powerful and sovereign God. He has the power to bring a resolution if He desires. "Is anything too difficult for the Lord?" (Genesis 18:14).

I don't have the answers for why tough financial situations persist. We do live in a fallen world, and that is a fact. The answer you need must come from God. It may be something as simple as His showing you that riches are the most uncertain things of all (1 Timothy 6:17), or it may be something as difficult to accept as His desire for you to take refuge in Him for a long time (Nahum 1:7). Regardless of the answer you feel acceptable, I do know that there is a way to find solace—waiting on God in prayer and patience, and in using your God-given good sense not to look for answers where Scripture isn't specific. "Yet those who wait for the Lord will gain new strength; they will mount up with wings like eagles, they will run and not get tired, they will walk and not become weary" (Isaiah 40:31).

Long, extended times in prayer, frequent pauses for prayer during the day, and patient waiting on God to supply the answers will renew our strength. That's a simple answer, but it's so hard for us to accept. I suppose we are all looking for a carefully laid-out ten-step plan to financial freedom. Sorry, that's not the way it is. But God's way is actually easier than that if we are patient. He wants us to come to Him and rely on Him. Most ten step plans rely on human effort. Only by trusting completely in Him and proving that we trust by our patient, prayerful waiting will we be brought to peace in the middle of our pressures. "For the Lord favors those who fear Him, those who wait for His lovingkindness" (Psalm 147:11).

Faith and Testing

Although their specific problem was more direct disobedience than anything else, the Israelites who wandered in the wilderness never cornered the market on testing. God still tests us because He still wants to know what's really in our hearts.

Peter wrote, "In this you greatly rejoice, even though now for a little while, if necessary, you have been distressed by various trials, that the proof of your faith, being more precious than gold which is perishable, even though tested by fire, may be found to result in praise and glory and honor at the revelation of Jesus Christ" (1 Peter 1:6,7). James exhorts us to "consider it all joy, my brethren, when you encounter various trials, knowing that the testing of your faith produces endurance" (James 1:2, 3).

Our faith is worth much more than money. God wants to see how real that faith is; the money doesn't matter. If we have to lose money or always be living on the financial edge in order for God to test our faith, then so be it. The money is worthless and replaceable; faith is not.

Sometimes God uses financial trials to do a little more than just test our faith. He may use them to bring others to Him for the first time or back to Him if they have strayed. It's amazing to see how money and the making of it keeps us apart from the Lord. Yet our lack of it so often drives us closer and closer to Him. It's almost enough to make us believe that there is something inherently wrong with money.

Mueller has said,

> If we, indeed, desire our faith to be strengthened, we should not shrink from opportunities where our faith may be tried, and, therefore, through the trial to be strengthened. In our natural state we dislike dealing with God alone. . . . The more I am in a position to be tried . . . the more shall I have opportunity of seeing God's help and deliverance.[3]

Elijah's Walk With the Lord

Elijah knew what it was like to be tried. The seventeenth chapter of 1 Kings relates some significant events in Elijah's life. When we look at these events, as we did earlier, the focus is usually on the miracles and what the Lord did for the widow of Zarephath. But consider the events from Elijah's perspective. This was early in his ministry, and he probably needed encouragement and strengthening. God did it in an interesting way.

First, He took Elijah to a brook. Every day ravens would come to feed him, and he would get his water from the stream. It was a daily provision. He only had enough food for that day, yet God provided.

Then one day the brook dried up. God's provision was to send him to a widow at Zarephath. But when Elijah appeared in her front yard, he must have thought to himself, "This is some kind of provision, Lord!" The widow was about to prepare the last meal for herself and her son. Elijah told them to prepare something for him (which they did not have), and he promised that the bowl of flour and jar of oil would not be empty (which they hardly believed).

That was indeed what happened. Every day the three of them had just enough from the bowl and jar to feed themselves. At the end of the day there was probably not enough for the next day. Once again we see how God provides for each day's needs, one day at a time.

It's one thing to be alive and have hope exhausted; it's another to be taken past what appears to be the point of no return. The widow's son died. How much more final can you get? If death doesn't create the end of hope for healing, then what does? But God brought the son back to life and showed Elijah that death is not the end. He is more powerful than death and is able to provide even after human hope is gone.

Elijah had been led through a series of faith-building events. Every day his need for provision and survival had to be met again. He saw God provide for him and two others. Finally came God's provision in a hopeless situation, showing His power over death. Elijah's faith was ready to face the challenges he would confront in his extraordinary prophetic ministry.

Our Response

What's our response to the tests God gives us? Will we be like Elijah and continue with a closer and closer walk with the Lord? Or will we be like the seed sown among the thorns—those who hear "the word, and the worry of the world and the deceitfulness of riches choke the word, and it becomes unfruitful" (Matthew 13:22)? God has a purpose in testing our faith. He wants to see how we respond when our own bowls of flour and jars of oil are perilously near empty.

Some time ago I began keeping a journal. (By the way, that's an excellent way to keep track of your progress and growth through trials. It also does wonders to help pull thoughts together.) Every now and then I'll write out a prayer. The two I've quoted below were written about two weeks apart, right when I was in the thick of some of my pressures. The first one was written just after I had jotted down some thoughts on 1 Kings 17.

Lord, You have kept me and provided for me. Now there are three—Karen, Nathan and me. You have provided for us too—and I thank You. What lies ahead may be more difficult—but as in Elijah's life they should be situations which will draw me closer and closer to You. Please let me respond that way—no matter what.

I must come to realize that all these trials and problems are not here to destroy me or make me bitter or cynical. They are here to teach me wisdom, knowledge, faith and dependence on You. There is a reason for these things. Help me not to be fearful because of them but look for the lessons and the opportunities.

Trials are not here to destroy us but to mold us. "Behold, like the clay in the potter's hand, so are you in My hand" (Jeremiah 18:6). God wants to use them to build our faith for His glory.

Freedom from Anxiety

It's nice to know that God will use our trials, but that doesn't always relieve the anxiety we feel in the midst of them. What do we do?

Jesus gave us some clear advice on dealing with anxiety. In the Sermon on the Mount, He discusses the fact that no one can serve both God and Mammon. When we get priorities mixed up, it's easy to be anxious about food and clothing. He closes His discourse on anxiety with these words:

> Do not be anxious then, saying, "What shall we eat?" or "What shall we drink?" or "With what shall we clothe ourselves?" For all these things the Gentiles eagerly seek; for your heavenly Father knows that you need all these things. But seek first His Kingdom and His righteousness; and all these things shall be added to you. Therefore, do not be anxious for tomorrow; for tomorrow will care for itself. Each day has enough trouble of its own (Matthew 6:31-34).

In these verses we are given three tips on dealing with anxiety, two of which we've already seen. The first one is coming to realize that God knows what we need so we don't have to "eagerly seek" the things that so motivate and drive our non-Christian peers.

The second point involves living one day at a time. We saw this in the way God worked with Elijah. Concern over what might happen tomorrow is the fast-track to anxiety. Mueller put it well:

> It is a point of great importance in the divine life not to be anxiously reckoning about the morrow, nor dealing out sparingly on account of possible future wants which may never come; but consider that the present moment to serve the Lord only is ours, and that the morrow may never come to us.[4]

Finally, we are commanded to "seek first His kingdom." Most of us have probably read or heard a lot of good definitions of the word "kingdom." And we've heard a lot said about how we seek the Kingdom. Standard answers include spending time with God, Bible study, obedience, witnessing, fellowship, and worship. All these are good and should be pursued with diligence. But the more I thought about how we should seek the Kingdom, the more uncomfortable I became with the standard answers. I saw so many people, including myself, who were doing those things yet continued to suffer anxiety. Surely we must be missing something. Surely Jesus would not give us a concept so important as this without also giving us a clear, workable answer somewhere nearby.

In looking at the Sermon on the Mount, we do see "kingdom" mentioned elsewhere. As a matter of fact it's mentioned in the very first verse: "Blessed are the poor in spirit, for theirs is the kingdom of heaven" (Matthew 5:3). That's nice—humility is a cure for anxiety. But that isn't quite enough. Luke 6:20 says, "Blessed are you who are poor, for yours is the kingdom of God." Then in Luke 12, Jesus repeats His words concerning seeking the kingdom:

> But seek for His kingdom, and these things shall be added to you. Do not be afraid, little flock, for your Father has chosen gladly to give you the kingdom. Sell your possessions and give to charity; make yourselves purses which do not wear out, an unfailing treasure in heaven, where no thief comes near, nor moth destroys. For where your treasure is, there will your heart be also (Luke 12:31-34).

Jesus has coupled selling possessions with seeking the kingdom. This is a remarkable and radical concept. Perhaps the only way to be free from anxiety and to really seek the kingdom is through poverty. That's what some feel, but that interpretation may be a bit extreme. What are we to do? Do we give away more? Do we give away all? Each of us will have to wrestle with this issue. But there is an unquestionable connection between the poor and seeking the kingdom.

Furthermore, there is no talk here about a simple willingness to live a different lifestyle. Too many have said that there is nothing wrong with money, you just have to be *willing* to give it up. Too many of the rest of us believe that. If we're only willing to give it up but don't, then nothing has been proven. Scripture is clear on the point that "faith, if it has no works, is dead" (James 2:17). James went on to say that he would rather someone show his faith by his works than show his faith without the works (2:18). Paul, when admonishing the Corinthians about their giving, said that their desire to give was useless without the completion (2 Corinthians 8:11). All this runs counter to the widely accepted theory that only our willingness to give up everything is important. I wonder if we would really be like the Hebrews who "accepted joyfully the seizure of your property, knowing that you have for yourselves a better possession and an abiding one" (Hebrews 10:34). How many of us would joyfully let someone take all that we own or cheerfully give it up? It's impossible to know without it actually happening. We ought to pray to God that if we can only truly learn to trust Him by losing everything, then allow it to happen—either voluntarily or not.

One other point about anxiety should be mentioned. When anxiety starts to run out of control, it can become fear. At times we will be able to pinpoint the object of our fear; at other times we won't. There may be no discernible object of fear.

Proverbs 3:25, 26 speaks to this:

> Do not be afraid of sudden fear, nor of the onslaught of the wicked when it comes; for the Lord will be your confidence, and will keep your foot from being caught.

Maybe Franklin D. Roosevelt was right when he said, "The only thing we have to fear is fear itself." Proverbs reminds us not to be afraid of fear. Note too that the onslaught *will* come. Scripture doesn't say, "The onslaught of the wicked *if* it comes."

Fear is a big motivator in the business world. Employees are motivated by a fear for their jobs. Companies are afraid their profits will drop or they will lose market share. Entrepreneurs are afraid of the collapse of their business. We are all, in some form or another, afraid of failure.

As Christians we must come to view loss and failure differently so that the fear of them will not create stress. Usually it's not so much the failure that brings pressure, but the fear of it. The prospect of loss or failure is frightening because we feel we have a lot to lose. If we had nothing to lose, then the fear of failure wouldn't be so stressful.

Like Paul, we should reach the point of being able to say,

> But whatever things were gain to me, those things I have counted as loss for the sake of Christ. More than that, I count all things to be loss in view of the surpassing value of knowing Christ Jesus my Lord, for whom I have suffered the loss of all things, and count them but rubbish in order that I may gain Christ (Philippians 3:7, 8).

Our faith must be in God's provision alone — not God's provision through success, investments, retirement plans, insurance, money, or jobs. Faith in God *alone* will bring freedom from anxiety. But if we put too high a value on the things of the world, anxiety will always be part of our lives. A funny thing happened in our neighborhood recently that had a lot to tell me about valuing the things of the world. There are a number of little girls who live right around us. One of them got a brilliant idea when she discovered money. She asked our neighbor's girl to sell some of her own items and give her the money. This little girl made a quarter by selling one item and brought it to the first girl, who offered to give her seven cents for the quarter. The deal was accepted. How can you make money giving a quarter for seven cents? Apparently, this little girl had convinced others on the block that a nickel and two pennies were worth more than a quarter. After all, that's *three* coins and a quarter is just *one*!

Money has whatever value we give it. Our society has determined that it has a particular value. God has other ideas. It's time we saw money through God's eyes instead of society's. Perhaps then we wouldn't be so anxious about it.

Faith and Deliverance

Even though God may lead us into failure, keep us in a state of uncertainty for long periods of time, or allow us to live without resolution of certain problems for the rest of our lives, He is still a God of deliverance. That deliverance may not be what we would have asked for, yet it is a deliverance. It may even be given to us in spite of ourselves.

Remember Lot when it was time for Sodom to be destroyed? Angels came to him to warn him and get him out of town before God's judgment hit. They urged him to take his wife and daughters and leave immediately. "But he hesitated. So the men seized his hand and the hand of his wife and the hands of his daughters, for the compassion of the Lord was upon him; and they brought him out, and put him outside the city" (Genesis 19:16). If it had been left up to Lot he would have stayed around. He even hesitated when the angels were there. But our God is a compassionate God and delivered Lot in spite of himself. If God chooses to deliver us, we won't get in His way.

God may also put us in an impossible situation so that His glory might be revealed through the deliverance. In Exodus 14 God hemmed in the people of Israel before the Red Sea. They were between it and the Egyptians. There appeared to be no way out yet they were right where God wanted them to be so that His power could be revealed. They didn't have to do a thing. "The Lord will fight for you while you keep silent" (Exodus 14:14). He did and they were delivered.

If you are hemmed in financially and there is no human way to escape, perhaps that is right where God wants you. Prayer, waiting, and trust may very well be all that needs to be done on your part. But over-spiritualizing may be a problem too, so try not to frustrate yourself by being too "spiritual."

During those times it's helpful to meditate on some Psalms. Here are a few suggestions:

O Lord my God, in Thee I have taken refuge; save me from all those who pursue me, and deliver me (Psalm 7:1).

Behold, the eye of the Lord is on those who fear Him, on those who hope for His lovingkindness, to deliver their soul from death, and to keep them alive in famine (Psalm 33:18, 19).

Many are the afflictions of the righteous; but the Lord delivers him out of them all (Psalm 34:19).

The kind of deliverance we are given may not always be what we expect. Often that's hard for us to take. We have too many preconceived notions about what God must let happen or won't let happen. But God is not limited by our expectations. He might do something that we never thought He could let happen.

For example, I've seen a number of wonderful believers go through bankruptcy or foreclosure. Years ago I used to think that God would never let that kind of thing happen. But He does and it is unquestionably a deliverance. Just talk to the folks who go through bankruptcy, and they'll tell you what an incredible relief and what great peace came over them when they finally filed. Clearly that was their deliverance.

Many of us also have preconceived notions about working wives who have little children. Again we think that God doesn't want that. But I have seen the deliverance from financial pressures that came about once the wife did go back to work. In our society this is often necessary, not to maintain a high standard of living, but simply to put food on the table. We should not exclude this from God's options either.

Finally, another type of deliverance can also be difficult to accept. We read about it in Isaiah 57:1, "The righteous man perishes, and no man takes it to heart; and devout men are taken away while no one understands. For the righteous man is taken away from evil." Death is a deliverance. It's seldom easy or painless, but God is sovereign and has chosen to remove His people from evil through death many times. His deliverance may not be our deliverance but His deliverance comes from His lovingkindness.

God's Mercy and Sovereignty

When we were nearing a very critical point in the life (or death) of one of our real estate projects, we were told by our lender to put up $200,000 or lose it. As we sat around the table discussing our options, it was interesting to observe the reaction of each partner. One was very angry, another was despondent and depressed, and another was somewhat more relaxed. Yet during that time I felt a strange sense of peace. It had occurred to me that since the problems with all our projects were so immense, intense, and unrelenting, God had to be in the middle of them. I know that's an odd statement. But I was absolutely convinced that God would not allow everything to get so far out of hand, in spite of all our prayers and efforts, without the condition of these projects being in the center of His will. I felt a peace that this particular meeting didn't matter and that whatever anyone might do to me didn't matter. God was in control.

Two months later we were delivered from that project. The Lord brought someone who put up the necessary cash, and we sold the project to his investment group. We didn't make any money, but we were free. God had delivered us.

That very day a tenant in one of our other projects filed for bankruptcy. The project itself was sinking deeper and deeper into trouble. One week earlier we missed an interest payment on our land. It was eventually foreclosed on, and we lost tens of thousands of dollars. But God chose foreclosure to deliver us.

Why does God use both painless and painful means of deliverance? Why does He allow one project to go down and another to be rescued? Why does one person succeed and another fail? Theologians and scholars have long wrestled with these questions. I am certainly not one to provide a new revelation. But at least Scripture gives us a way to live with the questions. Look at how David dealt with his problems:

> Be gracious, O God, for man has trampled upon me; fighting all day long he oppresses me. My foes have trampled upon me all day long, for they are many who fight proudly against me. When I am afraid, I will put my trust in Thee. In God whose word I praise, in God I have put my trust; I shall not be afraid. What can mere man do to me? . . . This I know, that God is for me. In God, whose word I praise, in the Lord, whose word I praise, in God I have put my trust, I shall not be afraid. What can man do to me? (Psalm 56:1-4, 9-11).

How could someone with such severe problems write words like those? Why did God allow those problems? I believe it was to show David he needed to fear God only. Building this character trait into David was more important than any situation or circumstance.

Consider the classic example of suffering—Job. He had to answer the hardest of all questions. It is the question that every serious Christian must confront at one point in his life: Is it possible to have faith in God even when He appears to be the adversary? Job asked the question this way: "Shall we indeed accept good from God and not accept adversity?" (Job 2:10). Later on, Job answered his own question: "Though He slay me, I will hope in Him" (Job 13:15). The question is put to each of us. Even though God slays us and takes away everything, will we still believe? Will we still be committed in spite of the adversity He brings?

This is such a critical point that I can't emphasize it enough. God cares more about our faith than anything else. Pleasures and pains, successes and failures, winning and losing, laughing and crying, finding and keeping, living and dying—all these things are nothing compared to our faith.

Job saw this very plainly, even more so at the end of his ordeal. His conclusion: "I have heard of Thee by the hearing of the ear; but now, my eye sees Thee" (Job 42:5). God wanted Job to see Him more clearly at the end of his trials than he did before they began. Job passed the test.

Peter writes that our faith is more precious than gold, and trials are to prove that faith so that we may give more glory and honor and praise to Jesus Christ (1 Peter 1:6, 7).

Paul must have felt like us too. At times the problems and uncertainties hanging over my head were so immense that all I wanted to do was give up. My motivation was at an all-time low, and I felt like everything I did was for nothing. I could identify with Paul when he wrote, "We are afflicted in every way, but not crushed; perplexed, but not despairing; persecuted, but not forsaken; struck down, but not destroyed" (2 Corinthians 4:8, 9).

God wanted to see how I operated under the intense pressure of being afflicted, perplexed, persecuted and struck down. It was a tough reality that couldn't be denied or thought out of existence with positive thinking.

However, God does have a purpose. He has not forgotten us. Paul went on to write, "Therefore we do not lose heart, but though our outer man is decaying, yet our inner man is being renewed day by day. For momentary, light affliction is producing for us an eternal weight of glory far beyond all comparison, while we look not at the things which are seen, but at the things which are not seen; for the things which are seen are temporal, but the things which are not seen are eternal" (2 Corinthians 4:16-18).

Our affliction is producing an inconceivable glory! Right now we can't see it, but by faith we must believe that it is there. We must keep "pressing on to know the Lord," even though He has "torn us" and "wounded us" (Hosea 6:1-3). Only by faith can we press on. Only by faith can we believe in Him when He appears to be our adversary. Only by faith can we surmount the pressures. Only by faith can we overcome the world. "For whatever is born of God overcomes the world; and this is the victory that has overcome the world—our faith" (1 John 5:4).

Conclusion

Sometimes we feel like we are just existing—plodding on and on from day to day with no purpose or direction. Life is a daily struggle to make ends meet, put in more time at work, or protect what we've made. Our anxieties are compounded every time we open the mail and wonder if there will be enough money this month to pay the bills. We can never quite leave the worries behind and rise above them to concentrate on what we know must be more important and eternal matters. The pressures block our vision.

Satan and society have tricked us. While we worry about mammon, we spend less and less time devoted to God. We are told to work and strive—make something happen. "Cease striving and know that I am God" (Psalm 46:10) has little meaning to the modern Christian.

Human effort will not relieve the financial pressures confronting us and lead us to financial freedom. As much as we would like to be able to control what happens to us, God has chosen another way. His way is patience, waiting, trusting, and faith. His way is peace.

Step #8 to Financial Freedom

When pressures mount, let God work the deliverance in His own way.

LISTENING TO GOD

Prayer

In 1844, George Mueller penned the following:

> Suppose I am so situated in my business that day by day such
> difficulties arise that I continually find that I take wrong steps
> by reason of these great difficulties. How may the case be altered
> for the better? In myself I see no remedy for the difficulties. In
> looking at myself I can expect nothing but to make still further
> mistakes, and, therefore, trial upon trial seems to be before me.
> And yet I need not despair. The living God is my partner. *I*
> have not sufficient wisdom to meet these difficulties so as to be
> able to know what steps to take, but *he* is able to direct me.
> What I have, therefore, to do, is this: in simplicity to spread my
> case before my heavenly Father and my Lord Jesus. The
> Father and the Son are my partners. I have to tell out my heart
> to God, and to ask him, that, as he is my partner, and I have no
> wisdom in myself to meet all the many difficulties which contin-
> ually occur in my business, he would be pleased to guide and
> direct me, and to supply me with the needful wisdom; and then
> I have to believe that God will do so, and go with good courage
> to my business, and expect help from him in the next difficulty
> that may come before me. I have to look out for guidance, I
> have to expect counsel from the Lord; and as assuredly as I do
> so, I shall have it, I shall find that I am not nominally, but
> really, in partnership with the Father and with the Son.

Another instance: There is a father and mother with seven
small children. Both parents are believers. The father works in
a manufactory, but cannot earn more than ten shillings per
week. The mother cannot earn anything. These ten shillings
are too little for the supply of nourishing and wholesome food
for seven growing children and their parents, and for providing
them with the other necessaries of life. What is to be done in

such a case? Surely not to find fault with the manufacturer, who may not be able to afford more wages, and much less to murmur against God; but the parents have in simplicity to tell God, their partner, that the wages of ten shillings a week are not sufficient in England to provide nine persons with all they need, so as that their health be not injured. They have to remind God that he is not a hard master, not an unkind being, but a most loving Father, who has abundantly proved the love of his heart in the gift of his only begotten Son. And they have in childlike simplicity to ask him that either he would order it so that the manufacturer may be able to allow more wages; or that he (the Lord) would find them another place, where the father would be able to earn more; or that he would be pleased, somehow or other, as it may seem good to him, to supply them with more means. They have to ask the Lord, in childlike simplicity, again and again for it, if he does not answer their request at once; and they have to believe that God, their Father and partner, will give them the desire of their hearts. They have to expect an answer to their prayers; day by day they have to look out for it, and to repeat their request till God grants it. As assuredly as they believe that God will grant them their request, so assuredly it shall be granted.[1]

I've always disliked "pat Christian answers." Nothing is more insulting than to give a pat answer to a difficult question. So when I started to write this chapter I was afraid that prayer might be interpreted as my own brand of a pat answer. I suppose in a way it is. I struggled with that for a while. There are so many tough financial problems we must face, it does seem insulting to say that prayer is the key to the answer. But it is, and the patness of the fact that prayer is the answer shouldn't blind us to its validity.

However, there is more of an answer than just saying, "Pray." What we do with our prayer times, the nature of prayer, how we respond when we aren't praying, and what we do with the answers God gives us must also be considered.

Answers

God answers prayer. I know that's hard for some people to believe, but I am absolutely convinced it's true. It's hard for a certain pastor in Minnesota to believe. My wife tells of a sermon she heard by this pastor. He stated from the pulpit that God does not necessarily answer our prayers—"Go ahead and pray, but don't rely on God to be the only answer to your problem." His son had been in Vietnam during the war. Week after week he asked his congregation to pray for that son. Pray that he wouldn't be wounded. Pray that he would come home safely. They prayed and they prayed and they prayed. The son didn't come home. The pastor has never again believed that prayer would produce answers. He stated that if you pray for a friend who needs a job, tell your friend you are praying for him, but don't expect your prayers to help him get his job.

Answers that are different from our requests are hard to understand. But this pastor wasn't the first person to experience that kind of answer. David himself prayed that his son would be spared. God struck him so that he was very sick. For seven days David fasted and prayed and lay on the ground all night. He poured himself out to God but the child still died. And do you know how David reacted when he was told the child had died? He "arose from the ground, washed, anointed himself, and changed his clothes; and he came into the house of the Lord and worshipped." His response was, "While the child was still alive, I fasted and wept; for I said, 'Who knows, the Lord may be gracious to me, that the child may live.' But now he has died; why should I fast? Can I bring him back again? I shall go to him but he will not return to me" (2 Samuel 12:15-23).

It takes a lot of courage to worship God when He answers us in a way that's different from our requests. But David's response was right. God is still God. David's life still went on, and he had to respond to God in some way. He could have chosen to deny His power and sovereignty, like the pastor in Minnesota did. Or he could acknowledge it and get on with life. Paul was faced with a similar problem. He had been given a "thorn in the flesh" and "entreated the Lord three times that it might depart from me." God chose not to grant his request. Paul finally concluded, "I will rather boast about my weaknesses, that the power of Christ may dwell in me" (2 Corinthians 12:7-9). Paul didn't let a different answer to his prayers stand in the way of his spreading the word about God's love, compassion, and sovereignty.

Even our Lord Himself had to face the possibility of a different answer. Before His crucifixion He asked God, "My Father, if it is possible, let this cup pass from Me; yet not as I will, but as Thou wilt" (Matthew 26:39). Jesus wondered if there was another way. Couldn't God provide an alternative to what He was about to face? But if not, He would go through with it. God's will was more important.

Jesus knew there were some things that couldn't be changed. Or as Numbers 23:8 states it another way, "How shall I curse, whom God has not cursed? And how can I denounce, whom the Lord has not denounced?" We can't pray against the will of God and expect Him to grant our requests. God doesn't work that way.

However, He will always give us grace. In Hebrews 4:16, we read, "Let us therefore draw near with confidence to the throne of grace, that we may receive mercy and may find grace to help in time of need." No matter what the answer may be, the grace to live with it is always there.

At times the reason why God gives us a different answer can be more obvious. James writes, "You ask and do not receive, because you ask with wrong motives, so that you may spend it on your pleasures. You adulteresses, do you not know that friendship with the world is hostility toward God? Therefore, whoever wishes to be a friend of the world makes himself an enemy of God" (James 4:3, 4).

These are key verses. James points out that many in the fellowship are asking and not receiving. He says it's because they don't have the right motives. They seek their own pleasure rather than God's glory. They are friendly with the world and therefore hostile toward God. We are to quit being so accommodating to the world and its values and draw near to God instead.

The fact that God doesn't answer prayers coming from wrong motives seems clear from Scripture. Even in the Old Testament we are told, "All the ways of a man are clean in his own sight, but the Lord weighs the motives" (Proverbs 16:2). However, we have somehow gotten the notion that God is our servant. We can call on Him whenever we want, tell Him whatever we want, and He will grant it. That's all done without reference to what's best for us or His glory.

Trappist Monk Thomas Merton says that one of the problems in prayer is learning when our efforts are well-directed and when they come from our own immature desires. He adds, "It would be a mistake to suppose that mere good will is, by itself, a sufficient guarantee that all our efforts will finally attain to a good result. Serious mistakes can be made even with the greatest goodwill. Certain temptations and delusions are to be regarded as a normal part of the life of prayer, and when a person thinks he has attained to a certain facility in contemplation, he may find himself getting all kinds of strange ideas and he may, what is more, cling to them with a fierce dedication, convinced that they are supernatural graces and signs of God's blessings upon his efforts when, in fact, they simply show that he has gone off the right track and is perhaps in rather serious danger."[2]

God's Silence

It's one thing to get an answer that is different from our request. At least that's an answer. It is more difficult not to get any answer. We pray and pray and pray. We pray by ourselves. We pray with others. They pray for us. We fast, we praise, we worship, we believe, and we expect. This may go on for months and months, yet we still see no answer. Praying for personal guidance in tough situations can often be like that. We feel like Habakkuk who cried, "How long, O Lord, will I call for help, and Thou wilt not hear?" (Habakkuk 1:2).

There are others with whom we can identify. Job: "I cry out to Thee for help, but Thou dost not answer me; I stand up, and Thou dost turn Thy attention against me" (Job 30:20). Heman: "O Lord, why dost Thou reject my soul? Why dost Thou hide Thy face from me?" (Psalm 88:14). David: "My God, my God, why hast Thou forsaken me? Far from my deliverance are the words of my groaning. O my God, I cry by day, but Thou dost not answer; and by night, but I have no rest" (Psalm 22:1, 2).

God sometimes seems silent when we think we need direction. And it is important during such times to tell God that we love Him and to keep up with our obedience to Him. This can keep us busy while we wait.

Waiting must have been a tough experience for the Israelites. They had to wait a lot. There was a cloud that covered the taber-

nacle. Whenever the cloud was raised up by the Lord and
started moving, the Israelites would move right along with it.
Wherever the cloud would settle down, that's where they would
camp. At times the cloud stayed over the tabernacle for just a
couple of days. They camped there for those few days. Sometimes the cloud would stay only from evening until morning.
The people would move out in the morning. Many times the
cloud stayed as long as a month. They would wait for a month,
then move on. There were even times when the cloud would
linger for a year. The people waited and surely they must have
wondered. Why would God have them move after a two-day
wait last week only to keep them for a week this time? Why did
He make them wait a month? What was He trying to do when
they had to stay in one place for a year? You can almost picture
the scene. Every morning people would crawl out of their tents
and look for the cloud. It was still there; God wanted them to
wait a little longer. "At the command of the Lord they camped,
and at the command of the Lord they set out" (Numbers
9:15-23). The movement was all in God's time.

Surely Martha and Mary wondered what Jesus was doing
too. Lazarus was sick. They sent word to Jesus, and what do you
think He did? Why, He rushed to Bethany as fast as He could!
Not quite. When Jesus got word that His friend, Lazarus, was
sick, He did nothing. As a matter of fact He stayed on two days
longer where He was. When He finally got to Bethany, Lazarus
had been in the tomb for four days. But the wait and the "nonan-
swer" were all to God's glory. Raising Lazarus from the dead
turned out to be one of the most dramatic and awe-inspiring
miracles of Jesus' ministry (John 11).

All of this should tell us something about "nonanswers"—the
timing of the answer is the Lord's. Yes, it is difficult to sit around
waiting and wondering why God doesn't seem to be doing anything. But we must come to the point in our spiritual lives where
we give the timing to Him.

Hallesby writes that God is

> unyielding on this point and that He Himself decides when and
> how our prayers are to be answered. . . . And if the Spirit can
> teach us also that there is no danger in leaving with Him the

time and the means of answering our prayer, our seasons of prayer will become in truth seasons of rest.[3]

I learned that lesson in a very interesting way. A few years ago I decided to keep a prayer list. I would write down my requests and leave room to note when and how they were answered. Back then I had the boldness (or audacity) to ask God to answer many of them within certain time frames. I wrote that part of the request down too.

Some time later I reviewed the list in its entirety. Immediately, an amazing thing struck me. Of all the requests that had been answered so far, not a single one was answered in the time frame I had requested. There were some wonderful answers but none during the time frame I originally desired. God taught me that He is sovereign over the timing of His answers.

The time constraints we think we are working under are usually self-imposed. Granted, we are told that if we don't "act now" we'll lose a fantastic deal. We see that a lot in hectic, go-go financial markets. A broker calls with a hot lead and says we have to respond now or lose this chance. My advice is this: don't go for broke in those situations. If you lose the deal, the odds are that you did the right thing.

I think specifically about numerous real estate projects that were brought to us by brokers. After the market began to collapse, I probably saw a dozen deals a week. I was always told to act quickly because the market would turn around soon. One year later most of those projects were still for sale at substantially lower prices.

Even when there is the pressure of wondering where the next paycheck is coming from or how we'll make the next rent payment, God's timing is still more accurate than ours. Whatever time constraints we have put on ourselves (or on God) they will inevitably create stress. If we leave the time when God will remedy our financial plight up to Him, the pressures will drop dramatically. "The more completely you cease being concerned about the time in which your prayers are to be answered, the more freedom you will enjoy in your prayer life."[4]

Requests Granted

Although God may delay in His answers or answer us differently from our requests, He may answer our requests just the way we make them. Jacob prayed for deliverance from his brother, Esau, and it was granted (Genesis 32:9-12). Hannah prayed for a son and God answered her with the birth of Samuel (1 Samuel 1:10, 11). Hezekiah became mortally ill, prayed for healing, and God gave him fifteen more years of life (2 Kings 20:1-7). Solomon asked for an understanding heart to judge the people and discern good and evil; God granted that and much more to him (1 Kings 3:1-13).

Throughout the Psalms we see wonderful and uplifting words of hope and encouragement regarding prayer:

> This poor man cried and the Lord heard him, and saved him out of all his troubles (Psalm 34:6).

> As for me, I shall call upon God, and the Lord will save me (Psalm 55:16).

> O Thou who dost hear prayer, to Thee all men come (Psalm 65:2).

> For Thou, Lord, art good, and ready to forgive, and abundant in lovingkindness to all who call upon Thee (Psalm 86:5).

> He will call upon Me, and I will answer him; I will be with him in trouble; I will rescue him, and honor him (Psalm 91:15).

> From my distress I called upon the Lord; the Lord answered me and set me in a large place (Psalm 118:5).

> On the day I called Thou didst answer me; Thou didst make me bold with strength in my soul (Psalm 138:3).

Our God is a God of answers and deliverance. It may not be now. It may not be next week, next month, next year, or even the way we want it to be. But God is there and He hears us. He has not moved, and He has not changed. He can deal with us the same way He dealt with Jacob, Hannah, Hezekiah, Solomon, and David. He still does.

Our Needs Supplied

One night, as part of our church's visitation program, I paid a visit on a young man who had recently been to our church. His name was David, and he had been a Christian for a number of years. He made some very simple statements about prayer that set me thinking.

David didn't make a lot of money, but he said he prayed and his needs had always been met. He said, very matter of factly, that he got up that morning and prayed for a job. A few hours later he got one. But he also commented that prayers aren't always answered. He explained that he didn't expect to get $1 million if he asked for it. He didn't need it.

God will supply our needs. Answers to prayer don't depend on our perception of their impossibility or magnitude. They depend on God's merciful granting of our needs. A job met David's needs — $1 million didn't. Was it that $1 million seemed too far-fetched to David or that he didn't have the faith because he didn't perceive the need? David certainly didn't expect the $1 million. But what about those who do expect it and pray for it but don't get it? The answer is that the need wasn't present.

God only promised us daily sustenance. "Give us *this day* our *daily* bread" (Matthew 6:11) doesn't speak for everything we need for the future. There is a tendency, as people or a society gets wealthier, to be more forward looking. Consider the poorest — all they are really concerned about is where the next meal is coming from. When those needs are met, the worries may shift to concern for next week's or next month's food. When we've reached a comfort level in regard to food we may start thinking about better housing. Then it's better cars, stereos, and other accoutrements of a stronger financial position. Next come worries about providing college educations for the kids. Finally, we come to the ultimate in forward-looking worries — retirement security. I'm not saying that we shouldn't plan for retirement, but the progression is evident. We're worried about things that are so far off as to be incomprehensible to most of the world. God only promised answers to our prayers for daily needs. Concern over the future shouldn't be such a large part of our prayer lives.

A Special Lesson

One other point about prayer should be mentioned. I am convinced that some things we pray for come to pass as we requested, even though they were not the best things for us. God may allow those answers for special lessons. Although they may bring great suffering and loss, He is still sovereign, and His purposes are usually made completely known sometime after the problems associated with that answer are resolved.

My partners and I prayed very diligently that the Lord would allow a certain man to join our staff. Clearly, God would have to work a miracle in order for that to happen. The man would have to take a substantial pay cut, shift to mostly incentive compensation, and enter a very insecure job environment.

The miracle happened. God answered our prayers. Unfortunately, it turned into a bad situation for everybody concerned. Although we learned some valuable lessons about employees (and I'm sure he learned a lot about employers!), we would have been better without him, and he would have been better without us.

An old saw goes, "Be careful what you pray for—you might get it." Ecclesiastes 5:2 says, "Do not be hasty in word or impulsive in thought to bring up a matter in the presence of God. For God is in heaven and you are on the earth; therefore, let your words be few."

Answers to prayers can be wonderful, different, long in coming, or exactly what you asked for but really didn't want. Just remember to leave room for the will of God to work in your prayers. Don't be hasty or impulsive; be willing to wait. God can use that waiting time to get through to you before He gives you something you'll wish you didn't have.

The Nature of Prayer

Part of the confusion over prayer and its answers comes from a misunderstanding of the nature of prayer. Why was David, after his son's death, able to get up and worship God? Why was Job, after all the disasters that struck him, able to say, "Blessed be the name of the Lord" (Job 1:21)? They understood the nature of prayer. They knew that a relationship with God had nothing to do with prosperity, health, or worldly security.

Arthur W. Pink, commenting on the nature of prayer, said, "Prayer is not so much an act as it is an attitude—an attitude of depending, depending on God."[5] Hallesby writes, "The fundamental law in prayer is this: Prayer is given and ordained for the purpose of glorifying God."[6] Somehow we've lost sight of those aspects of prayer. We are taught to pray expecting an affirmative response to our requests. When we don't receive our pleasure, the tendency is to get bent out of shape and take a few steps back in our spiritual walk. It never occurs to us to worship God, regardless of the answers to prayer.

When an answer delays in coming, some would tell us that we aren't praying properly. There are certain procedures, steps, and systems that should be followed. After all, how can we expect answers if we haven't mastered the methods? Merton calls these the "tricks" of the spiritual life. "The only trouble is that in the spiritual life there are no tricks and no short cuts. Those who imagine that they can discover special gimmicks and put them to work for themselves usually ignore God's will and his grace."[7]

God doesn't want tricks or short cuts, but He does delight in our prayers (Proverbs 15:8). Is it any wonder then that He would want us continually before Him?

When George Mueller's expenses were far exceeding his income, even for weeks and weeks, his response was, "But what was to be done under these circumstances? I gave myself to prayer."[8] Mueller's desperate financial situation drove him to pray more and more earnestly. Like the widow who kept going to the judge with her petition that was ultimately granted because she was so persistent (Luke 18:1-8), Mueller knew that God "delights in being earnestly entreated, and that he takes pleasure in the continuance in prayer, and in the importuning him."[9]

"Seek His face continually" (1 Chronicles 16:11). "Pray without ceasing" (1 Thessalonians 5:17). "If you seek Him, He will let you find Him" (1 Chronicles 28:9). "For Thou, O Lord, hast not forsaken those who seek Thee" (Psalm 9:10). All these verses and many, many more exhort us to diligence and persistence in our prayers. Even Jesus' words in Luke 11:9, 10 are built around the context of persistence: "And I say to you, ask, and it shall be given to you; seek, and you shall find; knock, and it shall be opened to you. For everyone who asks, receives; and he who seeks, finds; and to him who knocks, it shall be opened."

Before these verses, Jesus had just told His disciples the story about the man who needed three loaves. He went to his friend at midnight and was turned away because of the late hour. But his persistence was rewarded with the bread he needed. Thus, the context of Luke 11:9, 10 is not to ask once or twice and go our

way expecting an answer to arrive shortly. It is to keep on asking, keep on seeking, and keep on knocking. Only then will we
come to know God's will regarding our concerns, and only then
will He answer us according to His will. It's a struggle to be persistent, to keep praying for the same thing day in and day out
with no visible sign of results. Most of the time we either give up
or come close to giving up. To say "keep on asking" is easy — to
do it is a different story.

If we don't give up, there frequently comes a point where we
feel a little like Jacob when he wrestled with God (Genesis
32:24-29). These are the times when we pour ourselves out to
God and release our feelings in a torrent of emotions. The prayers
become so intense and draining that we know we have wrestled
with God.

There are those who say that this kind of deep, emotional
grappling with God is wrong. I am not convinced that these
prayers are always wrong. There are times to pour ourselves out
and cry to the Lord. But it is not our place to determine when to
do so. God initiated the struggle with Jacob, and He will initiate
our struggle with Him too. We don't just decide, "Tonight I will
wrestle with God." God makes that decision.

What good does this kind of prayer do? It's certainly not to
force God's hand and make Him respond. Neither intense will
nor fervent emotions are reasons why prayers are heard and answered. But in many situations we must reach this point of fervent prayer before we consistently begin to pray according to the
will of God. I have noticed that after these intense prayer ses-
sions God has done one of two things. He has clearly moved deliverance closer (either the kind I prayed for or another kind that
I didn't pray for) or He has given me the grace and peace to accept the present circumstances.

Let me briefly mention fasting and the nature of prayer. A
single paragraph certainly doesn't give justice to such an integral
part of prayer. However, others have written much on the subject so there is no need to dwell on it. Suffice it to say that fasting
is still just as important in our prayer lives as it was 2,000 years
ago. Merton has written, "Without trying to make of the Christian life a cult of suffering for its own sake, we must frankly admit that self-denial and sacrifice are absolutely essential to the

life of prayer."[10] The self-denial of fasting opens up a new dimension to hearing the voice of God. Sometimes, only through that kind of commitment can He really get through to us. I would urge anyone who is not practicing fasting to start doing so on a regular basis.

Prayer and Activity

How can we know whether to keep or leave a job, when to accept something as is or when to keep pressing on, whether to make an investment or not, if we should buy this or that, or which job to accept? Although most of us recognize prayer as an essential part of the answer, we continue to look for carefully laid-out plans of action that we can follow. It's part of human nature to want to be doing something.

If we recognize prayer as important to the answer but continue to search for other answers that downplay prayer, there must be something wrong with how we perceive prayer. Indeed there is. Too often, states Pink:

> when spiritual things are under discussion, the human side and element is pressed and stressed, and the Divine side, if not altogether ignored, is relegated to the background. This holds true of very much of the modern teaching about prayer. In the great majority of the books written and in the sermons preached upon prayer, the human element fills the scene almost entirely: it is the conditions which *we* must meet, the promises *we* must "claim," the things *we* must do, in order to get our requests granted; and *God's* claims, *God's* rights, God's glory are disregarded.[11]

We are quoted God's promises and told, "God helps those who help themselves!" No trite saying has ever done more to destroy the power of prayer or fly directly in the face of God's mercy and omnipotence. Scripture teaches just the opposite: God helps those who *can't* help themselves. He helps the ones who have tried a dozen times and failed, He helps the powerless, and He helps those who have been cast down and cannot lift themselves up.

Jehoshaphat knew the truth. When the Moabites, Ammonites and Meunites came to make war, he proclaimed a fast and gathered the people. He prayed, "O our God, wilt Thou not judge them? For we are powerless before this great multitude who are coming against us; nor do we know what to do, but our eyes are on Thee."

Then the Lord answered,

> Do not fear or be dismayed because of this great multitude, for the battle is not yours but God's. . . . You need not fight in this battle; station yourselves, stand and see the salvation of the Lord on your behalf, O Judah and Jerusalem (2 Chronicles 20:6-23).

Need I mention who won that battle? Hallesby has noted, "Prayer and helplessness are inseparable. Only he who is helpless can truly pray."[12] In Jehoshaphat, God helped the helpless.

Ezra knew the truth. He was going to take many men from Babylon to Jerusalem without armed protection. But he had told King Artaxerxes that "the hand of our God is favorably disposed to all those who seek Him." Consequently, he was ashamed to ask for troops and horsemen to protect them en route. So Ezra and his men "fasted and sought our God concerning this matter, and He listened to our entreaty." God delivered them to Jerusalem without incident (Ezra 8:21-23, 31). He helped the defenseless.

Hudson Taylor knew the truth. When this great missionary to China began his medical training in London, he purposed to live entirely by faith. He ate a meager diet, kept his attic room barren of comforts, and even refused to remind his employer of wages that were long overdue. He reasoned: "When I get out to China I shall have no claim on anyone for anything; my only claim will be on God. How important, therefore, to learn before leaving England to move man, through God, by prayer alone."[13] God helps those who can't help themselves.

In spite of both evidence and Biblical admonitions to the contrary, we persist in trying to rely on ourselves. Why? Human nature is part of the reason. When we don't receive an immediate answer to our request, we think that we must *do* something in order for God to hear us or to help the process along.

Another reason is our desire to be self-sufficient. Consider how we prepare for most of our meetings. First, we decide on a date. Then we try to find a place that will fit the size and atmosphere of our group. Next we line up a speaker and maybe get a song leader or musical group. Then we advertise, promote, and market. Finally, as the time approaches, we set up chairs, sound systems, video props, handouts, and anything else essential to pulling off a well-organized gathering. Immediately before the meeting starts we pray, *if there is time*.

A third reason we rely on ourselves is fear. We believe we really know what's best for us and are afraid that if we listen to God He might tell us otherwise. Hallesby has put it well:

> Now do you dare to pray, "Lord, teach me to pray?" That is right, be honest. You are afraid of trials and afflictions. And I believe that both you and I are willing to admit that we are also afraid of God. Pure instinct seems to tell us that God is going to deal harshly with us. And the same instinct seems to tell us that we can rely on ourselves, and that we understand what is good and what is not.[14]

Instead of relying on God, we rely on money, prestige, power, credentials, expertise, or skill. The efforts of most churches and their programs are no different from their counterparts in the unbelieving world. God isn't directing them; we are. And we aren't letting God establish His church on earth; we are merely planting our own religious structures on a foundation of our own values under a steeple that's nothing more than a facade. Without prayer we have built nothing. Don't misunderstand what I am saying. I am not saying that we should pray and always do nothing. Nehemiah prayed, then set up a guard (Nehemiah 4:9). There is a time for action. However, we have put too much of an emphasis on human acts at the expense of prayer. We must put prayer back in its preeminent position. Then we can pursue the right kind of human efforts. As Merton has written,

> The right use of effort is determined by the indications of God's will and of his grace. When one is simply obeying God, a little effort goes a long way. When one is in fact resisting him (though claiming to have no other intention than that of fulfilling his will) no amount of effort can produce a good result.[15]

It's time to swing the pendulum back to an emphasis on prayer rather than human effort, God's acts rather than our acts, waiting instead of action. When we have approached God first and relied on His efforts, then He can show us the right time to act.

Silence

Remember James 4:3: "You ask and do not receive because you ask with wrong motives." How can we discern our motives? How can we know what the right motives are? How do we know when God is ready for us to act?

The answer lies in a much-maligned and little-used commodity—silence. If prayer really is the means God uses to give us what He wants and the way that He can help us clarify our motives, then we should spend less time pleading and talking and more time listening and waiting.

But look around you. How much of your church service time is devoted to silence? How much of your Bible study or prayer group time is spent in silence? How often do people at these wonderful Christian meetings break into a spontaneous round of silence? Our churches are simply too noisy—with announcements and assignments, cantatas and conferences, meetings and music, programs and projects, speeches and sermons, and workshops and workdays.

Silence is lost because we are uncomfortable with it. Waiting before the Lord together or alone in silence runs contrary to our nature. Even our prayer times revolve around activity. From beginning to end we must speak with God. We feel like there is something wrong if we aren't talking to Him every second.

As a lawyer I can assure you that I've never had a client walk into my office, tell me his problem, then get up and walk out. He wanted to know what I thought, so he sat there and waited for me to respond. When I started talking, he got quiet and listened.

God wants to do the same thing with us. He wants us to tell Him our problems and needs. But when we're through, He wants us to be quiet and listen.

The Desert Father, Ammonas, disciple of St. Anthony, said:

> Behold, my beloved, I have shown you the power of silence, how thoroughly it heals and how fully pleasing it is to God. Wherefore I have written to you to show yourselves strong in the work you have undertaken, so that you may know that it is by silence that the saints grew, that it was because of silence that the power of God dwelt in them, because of silence that the mysteries of God were known to them.[16]

Some time ago I had the opportunity to get away to the Texas hill country. One evening I went down to the river to think and pray. It was an idyllic setting for prayer — the sounds of crickets and frogs, the soft glow of a quarter moon behind the haze, stars, just enough light to make out a slow current in the river, and the soothing sound of water falling over rocks a few hundred feet downstream. At the time I was trying to make a very important decision so I asked God to speak to me and give me direction. Suddenly it occurred to me that I expected an answer in the next five minutes! But God doesn't work that way. Prayer takes time. This is a crucial point that we have missed. In order to hear God's will we must listen. In order to listen we must wait. In order to wait we must take time. Sitting alone in the presence of the Lord for extended periods is what He desires.

The answer to a prayer may not come in five minutes, five days, five weeks, five months, or five years. Prayers are answered in God's time. Direction is given when He is ready. In Lamentations 3:25-28 we read, "The Lord is good to those who wait for Him, to the person who seeks Him. It is good that he waits silently for the salvation of the Lord. It is good for a man that he should bear the yoke in his youth. Let him sit alone and be silent since He has laid it on him."

Silence gives the Holy Spirit an opportunity to reveal things to us and pray for us, "for we do not know how to pray as we should, but the Spirit Himself intercedes for us with groanings too deep for words" (Romans 8:26). Paul goes on to write that the Spirit intercedes according to the will of God. Silence allows us to know that will too. Silence lets the Spirit intercede.

Many of our financial mistakes are simply the result of not waiting to first know God's will. The reason why we fail may have nothing to do with a sin or character short-fall. It could be that we didn't seek God enough initially. We might have responded too quickly or just put our heads down and ran forward without thinking or praying. God wants us to slow down and really seek Him. We should pray more *before* making a decision instead of after it. One of the biggest fallacies of so many of our prayers is that we lead right into the petitions without waiting to see what is the will of God. Before any requests are made we should follow Jesus' model and pray that God's will be done (Matthew 6:10).

After Saul died, the very first thing David did was to ask the Lord what He wanted him to do: "Shall I go up to one of the cities of Judah?" God said, "Go up," and David replied, "Where shall I go up?" (2 Samuel 2:1).

Those kinds of inquiries of the Lord ought to be standard procedure for the Christian. There's too much "pray first and ask questions later." It's time we ask questions first, then wait.

God will honor those requests. The answers may not be immediate and silence may be the central part of our prayer life for a long time, but eventually He will make His will known. It may be through a clear sense of His direction, the counsel of others, the way situations develop over time, or even a wonderful sign from the Lord.

I know a Mexican pastor who felt God's leading to build an orphanage. He began by praying that God would show him whether or not he was on the right track, and God had someone make a gift of the land needed for the project. The pastor waited and God revealed Himself.

Silence is not easy. It makes us fidget. We get restless. We may even feel guilty because we "aren't doing anything." But God speaks to us in silence. Be still. Let Him speak to you.

The "Pray It, Claim It, Thank Him in Advance" Philosophy

There is a teaching that has been fairly popular for some time and that has to be one of the most misdirected and destructive ideas about prayer that I have seen. It essentially says make your request to God, claim it as a promise, and thank Him in advance that He will give you what you want.

Rarely have I seen a philosophy come out of supposedly Bible-centered churches that does more to exalt and glorify man. We prance before God and thank Him for doing what *we* want Him to do. At most, it's our way of commanding Him to do our bidding. At the very least, it's a ridiculous attempt to psych ourselves up into believing that He will act in response to our whims. In reality, it is presuming upon God. Getting a favorable answer to prayer doesn't depend on advance gratitude. Persistence in that kind of prayer can only lead to deep discouragement and disillusionment. It's no wonder that those who continue in it always appear to be stressed out.

How did such a teaching develop? I'm not quite sure but it would seem to come from looking at certain isolated verses on prayer and ignoring some others. For example, it is true that David said, "In the morning I will order my prayer to Thee and eagerly watch" (Psalm 5:3). And, as we have seen, Jesus promises answers (Matthew 7:7).

However, we tend to forget that Matthew 7:7 is right in the *middle* of a sermon. We can't take this verse out and ignore the rest of the sermon. In Matthew 6:9-13, Jesus showed us how to pray. He showed us that we should ask for God's will before we ask for anything. In 6:24, He told us we can't serve God and Mammon. In 6:33, He said seek the Kingdom first. There are many other similar admonitions in the Sermon on the Mount.

Further, if we ask for fish, how could God answer us (Matthew 7:10)? We may ask expecting catfish, but He may answer with red snapper. He may even answer with chicken or beef. Suppose we unknowingly ask for a stone and thank Him in advance that He is going to give it to us. What would He do then? Hopefully, He wouldn't give us the stone.

Even when we move out of the Sermon on the Mount, Jesus adds some more requirements to the list of things needed for answered prayer. In Mark 11:25 (right after He tells us to believe that we have received what we ask for), He adds forgiving others. He adds persistence in Luke 18:7. Asking according to His will is added in 1 John 5:14. In John 14:13 He adds asking in His name. Abiding in Him is added in John 15:7. First John 3:22 adds keeping His commandments.

God doesn't always give us unrestricted answers to our prayers and thanking Him in advance doesn't mean that we are asking according to His will. We must still seek the Lord first, not only to know His will, but also to learn if there is anything in our lives that may be hindering our prayers.

Finally, if you *must* thank Him in advance, thank Him that His will shall be done.

It Hardly Seems Fair!

I had a law school professor who used to say this a lot. After the facts of a case were read and the decision was discussed, he would look out on his class and say in his most indignant voice,

"Why, it hardly seems fair!" A court's decision frequently isn't. Not only do hard cases make bad law, but hard cases often produce unfair results. The plaintiff should have won, but he didn't. The defendant shouldn't be held responsible, but he was. "Life isn't fair," President Carter remarked once. That's right—life isn't always fair.

God is hard to figure out too. Why was Hezekiah healed, but Paul wasn't? Why was Naaman the only leper healed in Israel during the time of Elisha (Luke 4:27)? Why are some Christians spared martyrdom, but others aren't? Why do some make a lot of money and others are always wondering where the next meal will come from? Why do you feel like you're in a dead-end job, but your best friend is always talking about how wonderful his job is?

I don't know the answers to those questions, but I know that they have absolutely nothing to do with the spiritual quality or effectiveness of the lives involved. God has other reasons, some of which are beyond our comprehension. But in our frame of reference, it doesn't seem fair. In this life we may never understand that. I know that's not a comforting answer. But I do know this: just as in faith we must all face the day when God appears to be our adversary, so in prayer we must confront God's apparent unfairness. This is the critical issue in our understanding of prayer. Will we still believe, will we still trust, will we still worship in spite of the apparent unfairness of God?

One man lives; another dies. One is healed; another remains in pain. One succeeds; another fails. Each of them did everything you would expect a righteous man to do. They prayed earnestly, persistently, and intensely. Yet the results were not the same. It hardly seems fair.

Perhaps all we need to count on is God's sovereignty. "I will be gracious to whom I will be gracious, and will show compassion on whom I will show compassion" (Exodus 33:19). When our prayers are answered, we should thank Him. When they aren't, like Paul when he realized healing wasn't coming, we must get up, go on our way, and thank God that He is still in control. He is still sovereign.

This is an extremely important point. We cannot have a maturing relationship with God or an effective prayer life without coming to grips with the seeming unfairness of God. We may never have satisfactory answers to our questions about fairness. But we must come to the point where saying, "It hardly seems fair," is not out of anger toward God but is more a tongue-in-cheek comment on life. At the same time we must acknowledge His sovereignty and His right to determine what is truly fair and certainly just.

Conclusion

Give ear to my prayer, O God; and do not hide Thyself from my supplication. Give heed to me, and answer me; I am restless in my complaint and am surely distracted, because of the voice of the enemy, because of the pressure of the wicked; for they bring down trouble upon me, and in anger they bear a grudge against me. My heart is in anguish within me, and the terrors of death have fallen upon me. Fear and trembling come upon me; and horror has overwhelmed me. I said, "Oh, that I had wings like a dove! I would fly away and be at rest. Behold, I would wander far away, I would lodge in the wilderness. I would hasten to my place of refuge from the stormy wind and tempest" (Psalm 55:1-8).

There are times when we can really identify with David. We feel like giving in and giving up and running away to where our problems are just a bad dream. The trials are hard, and we long for them to stop right here and now. Then we read on:

As for me, I shall call upon God, and the Lord will save me. Evening and morning and at noon I will complain and murmur, and He will hear my voice. He will redeem my soul in peace from the battle which is against me. . . . Cast your burden upon the Lord, and He will sustain you; He will never allow the righteous to be shaken. But Thou, O God, wilt bring them down to the pit of destruction; men of bloodshed and deceit will not live out half of their days. But I will trust in Thee (Psalm 55:16-18, 22-23).

Prayer is not futile. Through prayer, the mind of God is revealed to us. Through prayer, God becomes our refuge: "The Lord also will be a stronghold for the oppressed, a stronghold in times of trouble" (Psalm 9:9). Through prayer, God helps the helpless: "Lord, there is no one besides Thee to help in the battle between the powerful and those who have no strength" (2 Chronicles 14:11). Through prayer, God will relieve the pressures that are so heavy on us.

Step #9 to Financial Freedom

As pressures mount, let that be your motivation to spend more time praying, waiting, and listening to God.

We started this chapter with George Mueller and that seems to be a fitting way to end it. His practice of a life lived totally by faith is amazing. Perhaps we can all learn something from this description of him in the introduction to his autobiography:

> A single man, wholly destitute of funds, is supporting and educating seven hundred orphans, providing everything needful for their education, is in himself an extensive Bible and Tract and Missionary Society, the work is daily increasing in magnitude, and the means for carrying it on are abundantly supplied, while he is connected with no particular denomination, is aided by no voluntary association, and he has asked the assistance of not a single individual. He has asked no one but God, and all his wants have been regularly supplied. In these labors of love he has, up to the present time, expended nearly a million of dollars.
>
> We cannot resist the conclusion that if any one will undertake any other Christian work in a similar spirit, and on the same principles, his labor will be attended with a similar result.
>
> Whoever attains to the same simple desire in all things to do the will of God, and to the same childlike trust in his promises, may, I think, hope for a similar blessing.
>
> No Christian, though the poorest and humblest ever need despair of doing a noble work for God. He need never wait until he can obtain the co-operation of the multitude of the wealthy. Let him undertake what he believes to be his duty, on ever so small a scale, and look directly to God for aid and direction. If it be a seed which God has planted, it will take root, grow, and bear fruit, "having seed within itself." It is better to trust in God than to put confidence in man; it is better to trust in God than to put confidence in princes.[17]

TEN

THE TRUE CHRISTIAN LIFESTYLE

Contentment

It was the middle of April 1987. We were a few miles outside of Choma, a small town in Zambia. That night we had stayed at the guest house on the mission, and we were soon to drive back to the capital of Lusaka. A young Zambian pastor whom I'd gotten to know the previous week came over to talk for a while. I asked him if his son was any better. Just recently he had been put in the hospital, and the doctors weren't sure what was wrong.

There hadn't been much change. His wife was staying at the hospital all the time, but the little boy wasn't improving. I assured him of my prayers, he thanked me, and then we parted.

About an hour later I saw him again. I was walking along a narrow path between some orange trees and a banana grove. There he was, picking oranges. The friend I was with asked him what he was doing. He said he just needed a little food for himself and his family. They didn't have much to eat, and it sure was hard to live on 60 kwacha a month. We said nothing more and went on our way. What can you say to a man who makes the equivalent of $3 a month?

I saw him one more time. As we were about to drive away he asked if he could talk with me for a few minutes. I agreed, and we went to a quiet place by the guest house. He told me about his ministry as a pastor and how he travels around the villages to preach and witness to the people. Then he said, "It is very cool at night here, and I have nothing to keep me warm when I travel. Could you please send me a sleeping bag when you get back to America? We cannot buy them here." I told him I would ship one to him as soon as I returned. He thanked me and then made a final request: "Could you send one for my wife too? We are away from each other too long, and we would like to travel together."

The week after I arrived in Dallas my wife and I went to a department store to buy two sleeping bags. I guess that was the night reverse culture shock hit me. We found two sleeping bags — right next to seventy-five other sleeping bags, a few aisles away from hundreds of home appliances, and on the opposite side of the store from thousands of pieces of clothing. The contrast was dramatic. In Zambia I had left a pastor who couldn't keep warm or feed his family. In America I found a department store overstocked with items that are testimonies to our lack of contentment.

What came next was even more graphic. At the check-out counter on either side of us were magazines whose covers reported the latest in the "Holy War," the PTL scandal, or Pearlygate — whichever you prefer.

God's Priorities Versus Our Priorities

It took this African man with a sick child, a hungry stomach, and a simple desire to stay warm at night to show me that we have lost sight of God's priorities. We have been led to believe that the important things in life are bigger ministries, more television time, fashionable clothes, new cars, and a comfortable lifestyle. But these are nonissues that have distracted us from God's real purposes.

Many times I have been distracted. In the midst of my financial problems and striving for some semblance of financial security I received a letter from the Mexican pastor I was working with on a project for orphans in his area. As I read his letter I was struck with the fact that I was desperately trying to make money and far from being content while thousands of children only seven hours away from me were starving, both for food and for God.

I'm not alone. So many of us are worried about stocks and bonds, gold and silver, real estate values, the worth of the dollar versus the yen, whether our houses will be good investments, how much we can save, our insurance coverage, retirement funds, and on and on. We are not content in these areas where God calls us to be content.

There is another side to contentment as well. Although we may not be content where money and success are concerned, we are usually too content in areas of our lives where we should not be. Thomas Merton, while talking about the "good lives" of "good people" who have achieved some measure of security and status in their spiritual lives, said that "the 'goodness' of such lives depends on the security afforded by relative wealth, recreation, spiritual comfort, and a solid reputation for piety. Such 'goodness' is preserved by routine and the habitual avoidance of serious risk—indeed of serious challenge. In order to avoid apparent evil, this pseudo-goodness will ignore the summons of genuine good. It will prefer routine duty to courage and creativity. In the end it will be content with established procedures and safe formulas, while turning a blind eye to the greatest enormities of injustice and uncharity."[1]

We've gotten our priorities reversed when it comes to contentment. In evangelism, missions, service, and personal spiritual growth we are too often content with the status quo. Yet when it comes to striving for financial success and its trappings, we have conformed to the world. Instead of listening to Paul's admonitions to "walk no longer just as the Gentiles also walk, in the futility of their mind" (Ephesians 4:17), we run after a financial planner who boldly declares, "I believe that I can help you achieve the real American Dream—*total financial independence*. To prove it, put my first set of plans and strategies to work *absolutely* free."[2]

Is the "American Dream" synonymous with the Christians' call? When it's put in those terms, few of us would say yes. But in practice it has become our call.

Martin Luther once said that "if I profess with loudest voice and clearest exposition every portion of the truth of God except precisely that little point which the world and the devil are at the moment attacking, I am not confessing Christ, however boldly I may be professing Christ. Where the battle rages, there the loyalty of the soldier is proved, and to be steady on all the battlefield besides, is merely flight and disgrace if he flinches at THAT point." The one issue that we have ignored for too long is how we handle our money and possessions. Let me give an example.

Why was Sodom destroyed? Most of us would point to the account in Genesis 19 and answer that it was due to homosexuality, debauchery, or similar activities. But consider Ezekiel 16:49, 50: "Behold, this was the guilt of your sister Sodom: she and her daughters had arrogance, abundant food, and careless ease, but she did not help the poor and needy. Thus they were haughty and committed abominations before Me. Therefore I removed them when I saw it."

The abominations of Sodom were certainly part of the reason for the destruction. However, in Ezekiel the focus is on the fact that the people of Sodom did not help the poor and needy. The real guilt came from what Sodom did, or didn't do, with her abundance. Her debauchery came later.

Why hasn't this been widely taught? Most serious students of the Bible know what is written in Ezekiel, yet in regard to Sodom the emphasis has always been on homosexuality. I suspect that this is another indication of the way our society takes the focus off the real issue of how we handle our money. It's a lot easier to put the blame on homosexuals than it is to point fingers at those who misuse their abundance.

This is not to deny the seriousness of the moral issues confronting us today. Homosexuality, abortion, pornography — all these are clearly abominations to God, and we should do everything we can to stop their spread. But we have ignored a moral issue that is just as important — what we do with our money. That is no less of a moral issue than homosexuality or all the rest.

One well-known foe of abortion has said that the greatest moral test put to us as Christians is how we deal with abortion.[3] Abortion is an extremely important issue, but I do not think that is our greatest moral test. The greatest moral test of the Sodomites was not homosexuality. That sin derived from their arrogance and affluence. Likewise, a great many abortions take place so that a particular lifestyle may be maintained. Self is the god and materialism the dominant worldview. The greatest moral test put to Christians is how we deal with ourselves. Do we continue to lift up ourselves and *our* desires, or do we lift up God and *His* desires? The way we handle our money is a good indication of our answer.

Responsibility

We hear a lot about prosperity and success. If it's not motivating others to success, then it's probably an attempt to justify it. Our lack of contentment gets us so caught up in striving for success that we lose sight of our responsibility. Regardless of whether or not we are successful, we have a responsibility to use the resources God has given us. We might not have a big impact, but the responsibility is still there.

Two major areas of responsibility where we are typically too content have been related to missions and evangelism. Dr. Robert E. Speer, a member of the Student Volunteer Movement, wrote:

> If men (and women) are to have special calls for anything, they ought to have special calls to go about their business, to have a nice time all their lives, to choose the soft places, and to make money, and to gratify their own ambitions. How can any honest Christian man (or woman) . . . say that unless he gets some special, specific call of God to preach the gospel to the heathen, he has a perfect right to spend his (or her) life lining his pockets with money? Is it not absurd to allege that a special missionary call is necessary, while a man (or woman) may go on any pretext into any work that means simply the gratification of his (or her) own will or personal ambitions?[4]

We are not called to a life of discontentment in our financial affairs. The striving and seeking for prosperity have so overwhelmed our lives that we have lost sight of a Biblical model of a Christian lifestyle. What we need today are role models of balanced Christians—those who live simply and comfortably but not extravagantly. Those who are so content with their possessions that they are free to release them to others in need. That's true prosperity.

Jeremiah wrote that real prosperity doesn't come until we have acted responsibly. "They do not plead the cause, the cause of the orphan, that they may prosper; and they do not defend the rights of the poor. 'Shall I not punish these people?' declares the Lord, 'on a nation such as this shall I not avenge Myself?' " (Jeremiah 5:28, 29). Perhaps ours is really just a false prosperity.

Recently a large number of people in our church have been experiencing severe financial problems. One family got down to their last loaf of bread, and another couldn't afford to go to the grocery store. A number of families were forced to sell their homes, and many more have depleted their savings. Throughout all of this I kept questioning God. Are we meant to live this way—stressed out and under pressure? Or is He just trying to teach us something?

I think there are answers to those questions. Undoubtedly many of us have tried to live beyond our means in the past, and that is part of the problem. God is trying to take our emphasis off possessions and lifestyle.

Another answer is that He wants us drawn closer to Him. This is mostly through prayer, but it is worked out through showing our dependence on Him rather than on material goods.

He also wants to see how the Church responds. Part of the system God has devised to help people make ends meet is His supply through other believers. "But whoever has the world's goods, and beholds his brother in need and closes his heart against him, how does the love of God abide in him?" (1 John 3:17).

The lesson God is trying to teach is for those who also have means. The ability to make ends meet is frequently out of the hands of those struggling with their finances. The responsibility then falls on the brother or sister who can help. The lesson is for the body of Christ.

A final answer deals with whether or not we will continue to proclaim Christ. God is testing our hearts. Will we trust in Him regardless of the circumstances? Again, God speaks through Jeremiah to us:

> Blessed is the man who trusts in the Lord and whose trust is the Lord. For he will be like a tree planted by the water, that extends its roots by a stream and will not fear when the heat comes; but its leaves will be green, and it will not be anxious in a year of drought nor cease to yield fruit (Jeremiah 17:7, 8).

The drought will come and the heat will be on us. The pressures and problems of life will not pass us by simply because we trust God. But how deep is our trust? Is it deep enough to keep bearing fruit? Is it deep enough to keep proclaiming the love of

God and the Gospel of salvation in Christ regardless of our predicament? Can we be content with our circumstances and continue to glorify God? That's the answer. That's what God wants to see.

Contentment in our Situations

Numerous Scriptures speak to the issue of contentment. Paul tells us that he has

> learned to be content in whatever circumstances I am. I know how to get along with humble means, and I also know how to live in prosperity; in any and every circumstance I have learned the secret of being filled and going hungry, both of having abundance and suffering need (Philippians 4:11, 12).

Paul also writes to Timothy that

> godliness actually is a means of great gain, when accompanied by contentment. For we have brought nothing into the world, so we cannot take anything out of it either. And if we have food and covering, with these we shall be content (1 Timothy 6:6, 8).

Paul's words are reinforced by Proverbs 16:8: "Better is a little with righteousness than great income with injustice."

In Hebrews 13:5 we are admonished to "let your character be free from the love of money, being content with what you have; for He Himself has said, 'I will never desert you, nor will I ever forsake you.' "

In one way or another, contentment is the focal point of all the issues I've discussed in this book. Either we are too content where we should not be, or we are not content where we should be. The priorities have been reversed.

When John the Baptist was preaching repentance, some soldiers asked him what they should do. He told them not to take money by force or accuse people falsely. Then he said, "Be content with your wages" (Luke 3:14). How many of us can say that's not a problem? When it comes to work, we are usually less content with our incomes than any other aspect.

Even when we get raises, we aren't content. A sociologist at the University of Illinois recently completed a study on pay perceptions. He concluded that workers aren't satisfied for long after receiving a pay raise.

> Rather than end discontent, a salary increase—no matter how large—merely intensifies the belief that we deserve more. . . . And once we earn enough to cover our needs, we shift from trying to get by to trying to get ahead, which by its very nature is always just out of reach.[5]

Raises only make us want more. We are never quite content. As we have seen, work must be relevant to the Biblical commands to help the needy. The focus of work should shift from ourselves to others. Here is where we can be more content in our work. Let's stop worrying about whether we can always keep increasing our incomes each year and instead turn to making our work more relevant to God's call.

When we think about money, we must remember that riches are deceitful. Wealth really can't do what we've often been told it can do. Riches never let us rest from trying to acquire more riches.

Debt can also be a sign that we aren't content. There is a tendency to go deeper and deeper into debt when we are not satisfied with our present possessions, yet can't really afford to get new ones. We buy more stuff anyway and take on debt to do it. Likewise, in business too much debt may mean that we are growing too big too fast. It may be time to slow down and develop a more leisurely growth path rather than try to be the biggest and best immediately.

Our lifestyles also tell us quite a lot about how content we are. Wealth tends to create a selfish spirit in us with a premium on comfort and enjoyment. We want to be more comfortable and entertained. The contentment that we should have in our lifestyles is transferred to the spiritual realm. A comfortable lifestyle creates no sense of spiritual urgency. Affluence usually brings insensitivity to the needs of others, and it focuses attention on ourselves.

In the area of economics our society tells us that we should pursue our own self-interest. By our seeking personal enrichment, a universal prosperity will be achieved. So we throw away contentment and employ the drive of selfishness. That eventually leads us to the "move-up" syndrome manifested in our lack of contentment with present homes, cars, and other possessions.

A look at our values also shows us that we are not content. We value money the same way the rest of our culture does. Upward mobility and financial independence are just as important to us as they are to the next person. As we saw in Ecclesiastes 12, we have not come to grips with our own mortality. Thus, we spend our most valuable time on work and accumulating wealth. The church and our responsibility to win the lost don't excite us like our temporal pursuits.

Finally, we turn to the areas of giving, faith, and prayer. When it comes to these three we have been too content. Average giving figures from most churches indicate that only a small percentage of church-goers actually tithe. We are not giving bountifully.

In regard to faith, probably the most difficult thing to accept is contentment in mediocrity and failure. Are we willing to serve God if He tells us that we will not be successful? Are we willing to work for Him for years in a ministry with constant financial pressures and little reward?

Isaiah must have been a special man, for he did just that. When God commissioned him in Isaiah 6:9, He said, "Go, and tell this people: 'keep on listening, but do not perceive; keep on looking but do not understand.'" Isaiah probably thought these people would be hardened for just a short time. So, his reply was, "Lord, how long?" (v. 11).

Perhaps Isaiah thought there would be one or two tough years with a few people responding every now and then. Eventually a dynamic revival would erupt and thousands would repent. But God had a different plan. His answer was, "Until cities are devastated and without inhabitant, houses are without people, and the land is utterly desolate, the Lord has removed men far away, and the forsaken places are many in the midst of the land" (vv. 11,12). In other words, Isaiah's mission would fail.

Contentment in failure requires us to accept the fact of God's mercy and sovereignty. In any analysis of financial pressures we must believe that He loves us and He is sovereign. Then, even though He leads us into failures, we can be content. We can spend less time worrying about Mammon and more time thinking about God.

We will not always be content in our prayers either. A contented prayer life may become stagnant. More time will be spent in prayer and we will grow in the depth and intensity of our prayers. And we will develop a contentment to simply wait on God.

Conclusion

Our primary purpose in life is not to live in comfort and seek financial security. It is to glorify God and spread His Word. Glorifying God is an everyday action. It is to walk with integrity and seek justice, to treat other people with love and compassion, to maintain close communion with God and be immersed in His Word, and to spend time in prayer, listening to Him. This is a lifestyle.

Spreading the Gospel is also a lifestyle. It must be done on an individual basis day to day. But our responsibility extends beyond our neighborhood. We are called to feed the hungry, clothe the naked, shelter the homeless, and bring hope to the hopeless outside our spheres of influence. Otherwise, how would *we* have come to know the Lord had not someone crossed a cultural boundary long, long ago?

In a sense, this conclusion is not really a financial one. But that's the way it should be. Too many things are more important than money. God just uses our lack of money and the pressures created by that lack to get through to us. He did that with me.

There were times when the daily financial crises we faced took me from one emotional extreme to another. It was hard to handle, and at times I still don't handle it too well. But God wants to see if I can remain consistent and content in the face of intense pressures.

Perhaps God wanted you to read this book for the same reason. The financial pressures have been unrelenting. Each day you have to struggle just to make ends meet. You ask yourself, "What is God doing?"

Habakkuk must have asked that question too. But he knew the answer. Habakkuk knew that Judah was about to be invaded. He knew that the people were about to be taken into captivity. He knew that their suffering would be intense and they would go through some extremely difficult, almost unbearable times. But this is what he wrote:

I heard and my inward parts trembled, at the sound my lips quivered. Decay enters my bones, and in my place I tremble. Because I must wait quietly for the day of distress, for the people to arise who will invade us. Though the fig tree should not blossom, and there be no fruit on the vines, though the yield of the olive should fail, and the fields produce no food, though the flock should be cut off from the fold, and there be no cattle in the stalls, yet I will exult in the Lord, I will rejoice in the God of my salvation (Habakkuk 3:16-18).

Habakkuk knew that faith was not some fuzzy doctrine to be believed but a way of life. It is daily dependence on God. Habakkuk says that when everything has gone wrong, all possessions have been lost, and there is not even anything to eat, we still must rejoice in God. Faith says that God alone is enough. It says that we will be content with Him.

At the last supper Jesus knew He was about to go through terrible suffering. He knew He was heading into torture and a painful death. Yet He said, "Father, the hour has come; glorify Thy Son, that the Son may glorify Thee" (John 17:1). All Jesus cared about was giving God the glory.

A lot of you reading this book are going through some pretty tough times—no jobs, no work, no money. But God still wants to know this: Will you rejoice in Him? Will you glorify Him? In spite of everything, will you still serve Him? Can you say with David, "Whom have I in heaven but Thee? And besides Thee, I desire nothing on earth" (Psalm 73:25).

Step #10 to Financial Freedom
Learn contentment in those areas where God calls you to be content but don't accept contentment where he calls you not to.

MONEY MANAGEMENT TIPS

Should we develop our own financial plans, and if so, how? Is budgeting something we ought to be doing, and how can we prepare a workable budget? How much should we save, and where should we put it? What should we think about investing?

To comprehensively answer these questions would require another volume. But perhaps I can offer a few guidelines here that will be helpful. They aren't for everyone. As we saw earlier, Jesus' command to give away everything will apply to many. And for others, what God has called you to do with your money may make it difficult for you to fit into a traditional financial planning process. Nevertheless, I offer these general thoughts in the hopes that your thinking may be stimulated.

The Planning Process

Basically seven areas need to be considered in any financial planning program: giving, lifestyle, savings, risk management, investments, retirement planning, and estate planning. (I have not included tax planning due to the inherent technicalities of that field.) In order to begin the process we must first set objectives in each area.

The most important part of setting objectives is discerning God's attitudes. We have to be convinced that we know His will for us in each area.

Here lies the biggest and most fundamental error in financial planning. The majority of individuals and their advisors start from the premise that ordinary rules of thumb and traditional budgeting or investment advice can be applied to each person with only minor variations. For example, conventional wisdom says that for financial independence at retirement, people in their twenties and early thirties should save 15 percent of their income. From that point to the mid forties savings should be 20 percent. Beyond the mid forties a person should save 25 percent.

But does God really want some people to save that much or others to save so little? Perhaps He wants one individual to save less and give more, trusting Him for the later years of life. Or He may have a very special mission for another individual that requires a higher savings rate. God is working in different ways with all of us. Before we set our goals we ought to have a fairly good idea of what He wants. At the very least we should act on the best available idea of God's will that we have at the moment.

After discerning God's attitudes, you need to do some fact-finding. Find out where you are financially. If you don't know where you are, you can't possibly know where you are going. Write up your own balance sheet. List all of your assets on one side of the paper and your liabilities on the other. If you subtract your liabilities from your assets, you will have your personal net worth.

Then draw up an income and expense statement. List your monthly income and then below that record your expenses grouped by major categories such as housing, food, transportation, utilities, and so on. Subtract your expenses from your income to come up with positive (or negative) cash flow.

Another part of fact-finding is discovering your risk attitudes. What kind of losses are you willing to assume yourself and thus forego insurance? What types of investments are you comfortable with? You may feel good about buying bonds, but putting money into the stock market keeps you awake every night. Make sure you know what kind of risks you can handle.

After you've discerned God's attitudes and done some fact-finding, move on to setting objectives in each of the seven areas I mentioned. Objectives are important because they keep you from being sidetracked by "wants" that you really don't need, or by investments that aren't right for you.

In setting objectives there are three important principles to remember: quantification, timing, and priorities. By quantification I mean that objectives should not be nebulous statements that are little more than shows of intent. For example, don't say, "I want adequate retirement income." Instead, the proper phrasing is, "I would like retirement income of about $30,000 per year in today's dollars."

Timing relates to the time horizon on which you see your objectives being reached. These may be short-range, intermediate-range, and long-range goals. The short-range goals would be over a time period of less than five years; intermediate, five to ten years; and long-range, over ten years. They should be realistic and definite. For example, you would say, "I plan to retire at age 60."

Priorities should be set since realistically you aren't able to do everything. When you set priorities, you need to ask yourself questions like: Is protection of my assets more important than taking a certain risk to accumulate more? Is a college education for my kids more important than a comfortable retirement? Do I save for a vacation or for a new car?

Let me emphasize again that setting objectives must be consistent with God's attitudes. Before you quantify an objective, put it in its proper time frame, or give it a priority, be as certain as you can about God's desires for you in that area. Then, even if you are certain, be flexible. God may reveal something else to you later. Or He may have you change directions. Whenever you write out your objectives, write these words at the top of the page:

> Come now, you who say, "Today or tomorrow, we shall go to such and such a city, and spend a year there and engage in business and make a profit," yet do not know what your life will be like tomorrow. You are just a vapor that appears for a little while and then vanishes away. Instead, you ought to say, "If the Lord wills, we shall live and also do this or that" (James 4:13-15).

The Seven Areas of Planning

1. Giving

This is the most important area and was considered at length in chapter seven. As we concluded, the tithe is the starting point. From there you should build your gifts so that one day they will become a more significant percentage of your income.

If you are not yet at 10 percent and due to certain factors believe that you can't reach that point immediately, don't despair. Start where you are and gradually begin to give more and more.

Set a definite time to work toward when you will be giving the 10 percent. After you reach it, keep setting a higher percentage.

2. Lifestyle

This subject was discussed in chapter four. But now I want you to consider how to keep track of and control your expenditures by recording expenses and setting limitations. This is commonly called "budgeting." However, I almost hesitate to use the word "budget" because it has a bad connotation. To many of us, always trying to live within a budget can create paranoia.

Nevertheless, some sort of expense control is important. If your income averages $25,000 for forty years, $1 million will have passed through your hands by the end of the fortieth year. No business would think of spending that much money without a clearer picture of how it should be spent. Likewise, no family should operate without knowing how the money is being used.

Before you begin, don't forget to apply the three principles involved in setting objectives: quantification, timing, and priorities. Quantify by deciding how much to spend in each area. Put the objectives in their proper time frames by determining what you want to spend in the future. Prioritize the objectives by deciding the importance of each expense category.

The first thing to do is find out where you are. Remember the personal financial audit we discussed in chapter two? For a couple of months write down everything you spend — regardless of the amount. At the end of that time you should have a list of every penny you spent. Then develop expense categories for those pennies. There are endless ways to categorize your expenses, but you should establish your own since you can be more specific and personal. Obviously you will need certain categories such as food, housing, transportation, utilities, and clothing. But others will be more specialized and will apply only to you. For example, you may have medical expenses that are larger than normal and may need to maintain a separate category for those.

Once you've recorded your expenses and categorized them, prepare another personal cash flow statement. Like the first one you did as part of your fact-finding operation, list your income and expenses on a monthly basis. It should be interesting to compare the two statements and see how close your initial estimates were to actual expenditures. Then, subtract your expenses from your income. Hopefully, the result will be more income than expenses since families are not like governments. We can't print money!

Next, set overall spending limits and spending limits by expense category. This is what has usually been called budgeting. The limits make the budget. But as always, be flexible. There will be times when God brings something new or extraordinary into your life that will require an adjustment to those limits. Don't let it bother you. Make sure you've built the freedom to change into your attitude about the plan.

Let me add one other note here about "fixed" versus "variable" expenses. Fixed expenses are those that cannot be changed. Variable ones are those that automatically change every month. In my experience, very few expenses are really fixed. Even a house payment can be changed if the mortgage is refinanced at the right time. On the other hand, what is variable for some families might be fixed for others. Each individual or family is different and will have to decide what is really fixed or variable.

3. Savings

Should the Christian save, and if so, how much? At the risk of secularizing much of what I have said about money and giving, let me now add that simple prudence and common sense should persuade us that saving part of what we make is important. I do not mean to negate the fact that many of us are called to give away everything and save nothing. That is a realistic option, and Jesus demands that from many of His followers. But if you have sought the Lord on this issue and believe that He does want you to save, read on.

Again, the first step is to discern what God wants you to save for. If it is for adequate retirement income, then the rules of thumb I gave earlier should suffice — save 15 percent of your income if you are starting your savings program in your twenties or early thirties, 20 percent if you begin in your mid-thirties to mid-forties, and 25 percent if you start beyond that age bracket. These are hefty numbers but in view of the likelihood of a deteriorating economy and the probability that our social security system will not provide all the benefits you are entitled to, they are realistic.

There are other things to save for. Perhaps God wants you to start your own business. Another one of George Mueller's ten "means whereby the children of God who are engaged in any earthly calling may be able to overcome the difficulties" of business is by having adequate capital. Mueller recognized that many Christians failed in their businesses simply because they didn't have enough capital to start with. Of course there are many ways to get capital, but God may be calling you to create it by saving. If that's the case, you will need to determine how much you need, how much you can save, and how long it will take to build the assets.

An example of saving in the Scriptures can be found in Genesis 41:25-57. God told Joseph in a dream that the land was going to have seven good years, then seven bad ones. There would be abundance followed by famine. To protect the people of Egypt during the seven years of famine, Joseph told Pharaoh to save 20 percent of the produce during each of the abundant years. "And let the food become as a reserve for the land for the seven years of famine which will occur in the land of Egypt, so that the land may not perish during the famine" (v. 36). Pharaoh gave Joseph the authority to make preparations and the people were saved from famine.

From time to time, God may direct you to prepare for lean periods. Generally, if you feel that your job is at risk, having three to six months of take-home pay readily available would be a good idea. You might also try to save enough to cover your self-insured risks, such things as your insurance deductibles and minor car repairs.

Where should you put these short-term savings? For daily transactions, keeping a small amount in your checking account is as good a place as any. But don't keep too much there unless it pays interest. The rest should be placed in an interest-bearing account of some type. A money market fund or a short-term certificate of deposit would be all right.

There is a funny thing about savings. It seems that at every income level there are always a certain number of people who save and others who are always in debt. There are few excuses for not saving something, regardless of what you make. Set up a separate expense category for savings and build it into your budget. With a little discipline, saving won't be too tough.

4. Risk Management

Risk management is the attempt to minimize the adverse effects of risks through their identification, measurement, and control. In essence, you are trying to maximize the effectiveness of your premium dollars to purchase insurance.

The first step in risk management is to identify the risks. Make a checklist of all possible losses that could occur. Then put a dollar value on those losses. Make sure you are aware of both the cost value and the replacement value of the item should a loss occur.

Next, rank the losses according to their severity. This will involve putting a priority on those you feel most need to be covered.

Finally, select the method you want to use to insure the risk. There are at least five possible methods.

Assumption of risk is the most widely used. No insurance is purchased, and you simply decide to set aside some money to cover the loss.

Loss prevention activities should also be used where possible. For example, you may want to equip your house or car with a fire extinguisher or an alarm system.

Risk avoidance may only be an option for some people. If you can get by without owning something, then you don't have to worry about its loss.

Risk transfer may also be a consideration. That would involve leasing a piece of equipment or other item. The fifth method is insurance. There are so many different products on the market today and so many different ways to provide coverage that the only advice I can give here is shop around. Ask questions and talk to more than one agent or company before making a decision. The more people you talk to, the more answers and options you'll find. A little diligence can go a long way toward increasing the efficiency of your premium dollars.

5. Investments

Rather than get into all the various types of investments, let me give you a few general principles to keep in mind.

Diversify (also known as the "don't put all your eggs in one basket" theory). This is one of the oldest investment principles known to man, and it remains one of the best. Diversify by type of investment and risk. You might also consider diversifying by economic area and geographic location.

Buy low; sell high. That's obvious, but this is one of the hardest principles to stick to. The best way to know when to buy or sell is to watch the crowds — try not to follow them. Also, watch the historic trends. It won't be easy to follow this principle. As a matter of fact, it takes incredible willpower. But if you *are* able to follow it, you will come out way ahead.

Don't be greedy. A big mistake that most investors make is trying to hold onto something too long. Don't let an investment ride up forever. It won't. Try to jump off before it starts going down. Remember the tulips in chapter five.

Don't buy on emotion. If a salesman says you'd better buy now or lose the opportunity, that's virtually a sure sign that you will lose money. *Always* think about it for at least a day. Better yet, don't act until you feel comfortable. You might miss a few good opportunities, but you'll miss many bad ones.

Be careful with advice. A number of opinions are usually good if you are careful where they come from. Attorneys and accountants tend to be negative when they don't understand something. Stockbrokers tend to lean in the direction that will create the most commission. (I don't mean to criticize all attorneys, accountants, and brokers — I know many good ones. These are just general statements that you should assume are true until disproved.) As for investment newsletters, check their past performance. Some are good, but many are abysmal. There are investment newsletters that rate other investment newsletters. That's the best place to start.

Remember the bad times. Find the track record of similar investments, especially when times were bad for that type of investment. You want to know what the down-side is, and historical research can show it to you. That's also a good way to find out if your purchase or sell timing might be off.

Follow the sleep test. Can you sleep just as well after you buy an investment as you did before you bought it? I'll never forget a lady I had as a client back in my financial planning days. We had talked about a particular investment that I thought might be good for her and her particular situation. She said she would think about it. The next day she called me and said she decided not to invest. She just couldn't sleep last night. I understood. The sleep test is very important.

Although I'm not going to review the various types of investments, let me add one final point. The types of investments you choose depend on your objectives and the risks you can tolerate. Don't listen to someone who tells you to get into an investment without looking at your goals and your own particular situation. You can't invest in a vacuum.

6. Retirement Planning

Once again, take some time to discern God's attitude about your retirement. Perhaps He doesn't want you to retire in the traditional sense. Perhaps you will have income from other sources that He brings along. Maybe you will need more capital on reserve so that you can spend some time on the mission field. Each individual will have to respond differently to the prospect of retirement.

But as a general principle you might keep in mind that the amount of income needed after retirement without having to make a radical departure in lifestyle will probably be no lower than 80 percent of your pre-retirement budgeted expenditures. Once you've determined what that 80 percent level is, it's time to figure out where it will come from.

Check your proposed pension benefits, personal savings, or personal retirement plans. As for social security, that's anybody's guess, so I'll leave it to you how much to figure in. But assuming it is still there, you can estimate your potential benefits in today's dollars. More guidance is available from the government.

The difference in income between what you believe you need and what you think you will have is what you should start saving for.

7. Estate Planning

Estate planning involves directing where your worldly goods will go after you die. Not that I'm trying to drum up a lot of business for my brethren in the law, but a will is essential. I could tell you some sad stories about spouses and children who didn't know what to do when a family member died without a will. Don't let this one slip by. If for nothing more than your family's peace of mind after you are gone, make a will.

END NOTES

Introduction — When the Ends Refuse to Meet

1. This scenario is based on an actual family report. The International Association for Financial Planning has come up with a National Financial Planning Index. My numbers are close to theirs, but I've added a few things they somehow forgot about, such as another child and another car. See Scott Burns, "So Much for Financial Planning," *Dallas Morning News*, July 5, 1987.
2. "Earnings Plummet," *Dallas Times Herald*, June 12, 1987, p. C-1.
3. "Learning to Survive on the Land," *U.S. News and World Report*, February 2, 1987, p. 30.

Chapter 1 — Discern Your Calling

1. *The Autobiography of George Mueller*, edited by H. Lincoln Wayland (Baker Book House, Grand Rapids, Michigan, 1981), pp. 272-273.
2. Tony Walter, *Need: The New Religion* (Inter-Varsity Press, Downers Grove, Illinois, 1985), p. 114.
3. "The Agony of Unemployment," *Palm Beach Post*, May 10, 1982, p. A-9.
4. Lester David, "What To Do If You Lose Your Job," *American Legion*, November 1982.
5. Ibid.
6. "They Called Me in and Told Me Somebody Has to Go," *Chicago Tribune*, February 14, 1982, p. 16.
7. Terrence E. Deal & Allan A. Kennedy, *Corporate Cultures: The Rites and Rituals of Corporate Life* (Addison-Wesley Publishing Company, Reading, Massachusetts, 1982), p. 5.
8. Ibid., p. 16.
9. "Hard Times in Motor City," *Christian Science Monitor*, March 25, 1982, pp. 12-14.
10. Walter, op. cit., p. 51.
11. "Suddenly, the World Doesn't Care If You Live or Die," *Business Week*, February 4, 1985, p. 96.
12. Lynn Darling, "True Blue," *Esquire*, June 1985, p. 159.
13. Ibid., pp. 164-165.
14. G. J. Wenham, *The New International Commentary on the Old Testament: The Book of Leviticus* (William B. Eerdmans Publishing Company, Grand Rapids, Michigan, 1979), p. 319, n. 8.

Chapter 2 — Whose Is It Anyway?

1. Max Shapiro, *The Penniless Billionaires* (Truman Talley Books, New York, 1980), pp. 170-171.
2. Ibid., p. 18.
3. P. C. Craigie, *The New International Commentary on the Old Testament: The Book of Deuteronomy* (William B. Eerdmans Publishing Company, Grand Rapids, Michigan, 1976), p. 311.
4. "Child-Care Center at Virginia Firm Boosts Worker Morale and Loyalty," *The Wall Street Journal,* February 12, 1987, p. 25.
5. "Downward Mobility: Will You Have It as Good as Your Parents?" *Milwaukee Journal,* June 5, 1983, pp. 1, 2, 11.
6. "Wage Outlook: More Losers than Winners," *Dallas Morning News,* December 25, 1986, p. H-2.

Chapter 3 — A Harsh Taskmaster

1. "The International Debt Crisis," *Great Decisions — '84,* 1984, pp. 50-51.
2. John Eisendrath, "How the IMF Makes the World Safe for Depression," *The Washington Monthly,* February 1983, pp. 14-20.
3. *The Wall Street Journal,* October 20, 1986, p. 26.
4. Craigie, op. cit., p. 307.
5. *Vernons Annotated Texas Statutes,* Property Code, Section 42.002 (1984).
6. Derek Kidner, *Proverbs: an Introduction and Commentary* (Inter-Varsity Press, Downers Grove, Illinois, 1976), p. 72.
7. Ibid., p. 71.

Chapter 4 — Possessed by Possessions

1. Francis A. Schaeffer, *How Should We Then Live?* (Crossway Books, Westchester, Illinois, 1976), p. 116.
2. J. A. Motyer, *The Message of James* (Inter-Varsity Press, Downers Grove, Illinois, 1985), p. 169.
3. Ibid., p. 167.
4. Ibid., p. 168.
5. Ibid., p. 170.
6. Ibid., p. 171.
7. J. A. Motyer, *The Message of Amos* (Inter-Varsity Press, Downers Grove, Illinois, 1974), p. 145.
8. David Riesman, *The Lonely Crowd* (Yale University Press, New Haven, Connecticut, 1968), p. 228.
9. John Galbraith, *The New Industrial State* (Houghton Mifflin Company, Boston, 1967), p. 273.
10. John O'Toole, "What Advertising Is — And Isn't," *Across the Board,* April 1982.
11. The story of how cigarette companies got women to smoke is told in "A Hard Look — Seduced by Smoking Psychology," *San Francisco Examiner & Chronicle,* August 21, 1983, pp. A-1, A-18.
12. Richard J. Foster, *Freedom of Simplicity* (Harper & Row Publishers, San Francisco, 1981), p. 115.

13. These questions were suggested in D. G. Kehl, "How to Read an Ad: Learning to Read Between the Lies," *English Journal*, October 1983.
14. Mueller, op. cit., pp. 288-289.
15. Kehl, op. cit.
16. Glenna Whitley, "Breakthrough in Pantyhose? Firm Guarantees No-run Stockings with a Sheer Quality," *Dallas Morning News*, October 15, 1986, pp. 1-C, 12-C.
17. Len Feldman, "Here Comes DAT," *Popular Science*, August 1986, p. 82.
18. Mueller, op. cit., p. 271.
19. These first two points are from Mueller, op. cit., pp. 287-290.

Chapter 5 — The Gospel of Self-Interest

1. Charles Mackay, *Extraordinary Popular Delusions and the Madness of Crowds* (The Noonday Press, U.S.A., 1962), p. 89. The first printing was by Richard Bentley, London, 1841.
2. Ibid., p. 94.
3. Ibid., p. 95.
4. Ibid.
5. Ibid.
6. Ibid., p. 94.
7. John Maynard Keynes, *The General Theory of Employment Interest and Money* (Harcourt, Brace and Co., New York, 1936), p. 383.
8. Karl Marx & Friedrich Engels, *The Communist Manifesto* (Washington Square Press, New York, 1972). The first edition was in German, published in 1848.
9. Marx said that the "theory of the Communists may be summed up in the single phrase: Abolition of private property." Ibid., p. 82.
10. Ibid., p. 94.
11. Walter, op. cit., p. 127.
12. Address: "The European Communist Parties: The Communists Remain Revolutionaries," by Leonid Brezhnev, General Secretary of the Communist Party of the Soviet Union. Delivered at the Conference of European Communist and Worker's Parties, East Berlin, German Democratic Republic, June 29, 1976. Published in *Vital Speeches of the Day*, August 1, 1976, pp. 610-616.
13. Kevin Brown, "Report from Luanda: A New Angolan Society," *Nation*, July 17, 1976, pp. 42-46.
14. Ann Crittenden, "The Cuban Economy: How It Works," *New York Times*, December 18, 1977, section III, p. 1.
15. John Kenneth Galbraith, *The Age of Uncertainty* (Houghton Mifflin Company, Boston, 1977), p. 40.
16. E. F. Schumacher, *Small Is Beautiful* (Harper & Row Publishers, New York, 1973), p. 29.
17. Quoted in Louis O. Kelso & Mortimer J. Adler, *The Capitalist Manifesto* (Greenwood Press, Westport, Connecticut, 1958), p. 7.
18. Thomas F. O'Boyle and Philip Revzin, "Frugal Foreigners: To the Dismay of U.S., Consumers in Europe Resist Spending Spree," *The Wall Street Journal*, December 17, 1986, p. 1.
19. Ibid.
20. Ibid.
21. Ibid.
22. Schumacher, op. cit., p. 46.

23. Ibid., p. 240.
24. Quoted in George Gilder, *Wealth and Poverty* (Bantam Books, New York, 1981), p. 278, n. 3.
25. Will and Ariel Durant, *The Lessons of History* (Simon and Schuster, New York, 1968), p. 55.
26. Richard Reeves, "Domestic Political Power Erodes as World-Market Capitalism Rises," *The Atlanta Constitution*, November 28, 1986, p. 23-A.
27. "How the Market Is Rigged Against You," *U.S. News & World Report*, December 1, 1986, p. 45.
28. Ibid.
29. Walter Heller, "Halting, Hesitant, Haunted," *The Wall Street Journal*, December 12, 1986.
30. Jeffrey Zaslow, "Jim's Saga: Homeless Man Haunts A Gentrified Enclave, Baffling Its Residents," *The Wall Street Journal*, December 1, 1986, p. 1.
31. Heller, op. cit.

Chapter 6 — Whatever Happened to Integrity?

1. Mackay, op. cit., p. 50.
2. Ibid., p. 52.
3. Ibid., pp. 55-56.
4. Ibid., p. 71.
5. "The Class of 1990," *Forbes,* December 1, 1986, p. 10.
6. "How the Market Is Rigged Against You," op. cit., p. 48.
7. Ibid., p. 49.
8. Schumacher, op. cit., p. 31.
9. Walter, op. cit., p. 151.
10. Bob Greene, "What Makes a 'Hero' in Our Society," *Dallas Morning News*, December 31, 1986.
11. Schaeffer, op. cit., p. 205.
12. Ibid.
13. Gilder, op. cit., p. 132.
14. Ibid.
15. Ibid.
16. Kelso & Adler, op. cit., p. 159.
17. Gilder, op. cit., p. 176.
18. Norval Geldenhuys, *The New International Commentary on the New Testament: The Gospel of Luke* (William B. Eerdmans Publishing Company, Grand Rapids, Michigan, 1979), p. 419, n. 14.
19. Christine Wicker, "Socialists in Dallas: A Unique Party Crowd," *Dallas Morning News*, December 22, 1986, p. 2-C.
20. J. Christy Wilson, Jr., *Today's Tentmakers* (Tyndale House Publishers, Inc., Wheaton, Illinois, 1979), p. 39.
21. Ibid.
22. Derek Kidner, *A Time to Mourn and A Time to Dance: The Message of Ecclesiastes* (Inter-Varsity Press, Downers Grove, Illinois, 1976), p. 103.
23. Ibid, p. 104.
24. Vernon C. Grounds, "Faith to Face Failure, Or What's So Great About Success?" *Christianity Today*, December 9, 1977.
25. Ibid.
26. Quoted in Galbraith, op. cit., p. 45.

27. Ibid.
28. Ibid., p. 46.
29. Kelso & Adler, op. cit., p. 159.
30. Richard Behar, "The Special Talent of Paul Bilzerian," *Forbes*, December 15, 1986, p. 41.
31. Janice C. Simpson, "Business Schools—and Students—Want to Talk Only About Success," *The Wall Street Journal*, December 15, 1986, p. 29.
32. Joanne Lipman, "In Times of Trouble, Candor Is Often the First Casualty," *The Wall Street Journal*, December 15, 1986, p. 30.
33. Ibid.
34. Ibid.
35. Ibid.
36. Ibid.

Chapter 7—"Let Each One of You Put Aside and Save"

1. Frank Gaebelein, "Heeding the Whole Counsel of God," *Christianity Today*, October 2, 1981, p. 29.

Chapter 8—"Do Not Be Anxious for Tomorrow"

1. Grounds, op. cit., p. 12.
2. Mueller, op. cit., p. 408.
3. Ibid., p. 237.
4. Ibid., p. 389.

Chapter 9—Listening to God

1. Mueller, op. cit., pp. 268-269.
2. Thomas Merton, *Contemplative Prayer* (Image Books, Garden City, New York, 1971), p. 35.
3. O. Hallesby, *Prayer* (Augsburg Publishing House, Minneapolis, Minnesota, 1975), p. 52.
4. Ibid., p. 172.
5. Arthur W. Pink, *The Sovereignty of God* (Baker Book House, Grand Rapids, Michigan, 1979), p. 176.
6. Hallesby, op. cit., p. 127.
7. Merton, op. cit., pp. 36-37.
8. Mueller, p. 391.
9. Ibid., p. 337.
10. Merton, op. cit., p. 72.
11. Pink, op. cit., p. 165.
12. Hallesby, op. cit., p. 17.
13. Ruth A. Tucker, *From Jerusalem to Irian Jaya* (Academie Books, Grand Rapids, Michigan, 1983), p. 174.
14. Hallesby, op. cit., p. 161.
15. Merton, op. cit., p. 36.
16. Ibid., p. 42.
17. Mueller, op. cit., pp. xxiv, xxviii, xxix-xxx.

Chapter 10 — The True Christian Lifestyle

1. Merton, op. cit., pp. 103-104.
2. This was on the front of an envelope I received advertising Sylvia Porter's *Personal Finance* magazine.
3. Francis A. Schaeffer and C. Everett Koop, *Whatever Happened to the Human Race?* (Fleming H. Revell Company, Old Tappan, New Jersey, 1979), p. 195.
4. From a message written by Dr. Robert E. Speer entitled "What Constitutes a Missionary Call," quoted in an Inter-Varsity Christian Fellowship letter from John E. Kyle, March 31, 1987.
5. "Pay Raises Don't Satisfy Workers for Long, a Sociologist Says," *Wall Street Journal,* January 20, 1987, p. 1.

COLOPHON

The typeface for the text of this book is *Baskerville*. Its creator, John Baskerville (1706-1775), broke with tradition to reflect in his type the rounder, yet more sharply cut lettering of eighteenth-century stone inscriptions and copy books. The type foreshadows modern design in such novel characteristics as the increase in contrast between thick and thin strokes and the shifting of stress from the diagonal to the vertical strokes. Realizing that this new style of letter would be most effective if cleanly printed on smooth paper with genuinely black ink, he built his own presses, developed a method of hot-pressing the printed sheet to a smooth, glossy finish, and experimented with special inks. However, Baskerville did not enter into general commercial use in England until 1923.

Substantive editing by George Grant
Copy editing by Dimples Kellogg
Cover design by Kent Puckett Associates, Atlanta, Georgia
Typography by Thoburn Press, Tyler, Texas
Printed and bound by Maple-Vail Book Manufacturing Group
Manchester, Pennsylvania
Cover Printing by Weber Graphics, Chicago, Illinois